**Praise for Buy**

"*Buyer-Centered Selling* is a practical
who want to embrace modern buying ..... ... ..... ..... and customer engagement processes. Tom and Tom (aka The Toms) have done a great job explaining and visualizing a step-by-step path with very thoughtful questions to help our sellers solve a buyer's most urgent and prioritized business problems. I expect the book to become the foundation of many leading sales organization's go-to-market and sales enablement strategies."

**Elay Cohen,**
CEO and Co-Founder SalesHood,
Author of *SalesHood* and *Enablement Mastery*

"If you loved *The Seller's Challenge,* you're going to love this book even MORE! The world has changed; you know it already, and everyone talks about it. Unfortunately, very few people talk about the adaptation needed, and less talk about the habits you should change. Tom and Tom nail the five habits you should develop in order to have more success in sales.

Read this book if you want to have more sales success, and more importantly, if you want to help the customer buy. Get ready for a new, refreshing approach. Learn how to do customer research, and how to connect, create more opportunities, differentiate yourself and sell to your buyer's behavioral style.

I love this book, and I bet you will love it too!"

**Lahat Tzvi,**
CEO of Tfisot—Sales Consulting Group
Named as One of the Top 50 Expert World Sales Consultants

"Buyer-centered selling is an approach that is gaining momentum, and with good reason. Faced with today's complex B2B buying environments, anyone who fails to adopt a customer-centric mindset will inevitably fail as a salesperson. The authors have done an excellent job of pulling together the latest thinking on B2B buying behaviours and guiding salespeople in what they need to do to win in an increasingly complex and non-linear world."

**Bob Apollo,**
Founder Inflexion-Point Strategy Partners

"We all too often say that we need to align the sales process to the customer's journey, but do we really know how to accomplish that? Tom Williams and Tom Saine's *Buyer Centered Selling* provides the detailed road map for turning that objective into reality."

**Jim Dickie,**
Partner, Sales Mastery

"*Buyer Centered Selling* is the most detailed sales book I have read on the mission critical topic of knowing your buyer's journey. The book is packed with stories, evidence and tips on being buyer aware and using that to be a more successful sales professional. One of sales' biggest failings is not addressing the buyer enough in our sales process, this book addresses that challenge head on. Every salesperson and sales leader can learn from the insights in this book."

**Mark Welch,**
Author of *The Street Savvy Sales Leader,*
Founder of Street Savvy Sales Leadership

"In every complex profession, the best control the controllables with an unquenchable thirst for learning and skill development. With the complexities of the selling profession inflating at an accelerating pace, this book is an essential toolkit for anyone seeking to stay sharp, relevant and on top of their game. With the advent of the Information Age followed closely by the Digital Age, buyers still need sellers, but in an ever-changing way. The winning sales professionals are in a constant state of unlearning, modifying and relearning habits in order to stay on top. This book will find itself on many bookshelves as a fantastic source for mastering the evolving craft of the selling profession."

**Todd Caponi,**
Author of *The Transparency Sale*

"Insightful, focused and action-oriented guide to focus your selling skills on the most important person in the selling narrative, the buyer. Buyer centered selling will elevate your sales performance with focus and execution of its core principles."

**Mark J. Reis,**
Vice President of Sales
Anesthesia and Emergency Medicine, Teleflex Incorporated

"Tom and Tom take the complexity of any style of complete selling methodology that you are used to and turn it on its ear 180 degrees—flipping every aspect of selling to look at it through the customer's lens. Each of what you might previously have thought of as your own sales stages or phases are played back to align them with what the customer is going through, providing prescriptive advice and templates to evaluate how you might change your perspective.

In today's world it is the customer who makes the sale, not the sales team—and *Buyer Centered Selling* helps provide a framework for "crossing that chasm."

**Rich Blakeman,**
Former Sales VP and Managing Director
Miller Heiman Group

"*Buyer-Centered Selling* is the MBA you need for how to win over the complex buying team. Read this book to learn how to deliver compelling value statements that appeal to each buyer type. Includes helpful tools for applying the approach to win bigger deals!"

**Kevin F. Davis,**
Author of *The Sales Manager's Guide to Greatness* and *Slow Down, Sell Faster*

"What's the ultimate selling superpower? Confidence? Determination? Likeability? Questioning and listening skills? Storytelling? My vote is for mind reading. *Buyer-Centered Selling* is the ultimate textbook on mind-reading for the modern seller. Williams and Saine combine decades of buying and selling experience with industry best practice to guide sellers on the journey to reach a meeting of minds in the complex sale."

**Mike Adams,**
CEO, The Story Leader
Author of *Seven Stories Every Salesperson Must Tell*

"Who does your buyer need you to be? It's easy to make assumptions when attempting to answer this question. *Buyer-Centered Selling* thoroughly examines this concept and encourages you to think about your sales process from every angle. This is a tremendous resource for anyone in B2B sales."

**Jeff Bajorek,**
Author of *The Five Forgotten Fundamentals of Prospecting*
Host of *The Why & The Buy Podcast*

"One reason I specialize in helping salespeople to sell better at the "C" Level is that it's comparatively simple—not easy, but simple. But as Tom and Tom demonstrate in this book the entire B2B buy/sell process is extremely complex and is becoming ever more so. It takes true genius to describe such a complicated process in simple, easy to understand language; to explain how to navigate the process clearly and concisely, to incorporate tried, tested and sometimes forgotten sales approaches into the modern age and to distill their insights and research into an easily digestible offering.

I've read many sales books that leave me more confused than when I started. This book does the opposite—it gives clear, easy to follow ideas, steps and explanations that will help every salesperson steer their way through the complexities of big ticket B2B sales in the digital age. It also possesses a quality that all great business books share—it's not only amazingly instructive, it's an easy and enjoyable read."

**Steve Hall,**
Managing Director, Executive Sales Coaching Australia

"*Buyer-Centered Selling* is a very timely and welcome addition to the sales canon. The concept of 'buyer enablement' has trended strongly in sales thought leadership circles for the past couple of years and for good reason. With customers overwhelmed with more information than ever before and faced with more internal challenges to get projects or purchases approved they need all the help they can get. This is the first book that squarely addresses this topic and provides a fantastic guide for sellers and sales leadership on the need to adapt a buyer-centered approach and how to go about it. Drawing on their decades of real world experience the authors give us lots of practical detail as well as the high-level concepts. Well done Thomas Williams and Thomas Saine on this ground-breaking work."

**Steven Norman,**
Founder of Growth Acumen
Author of *Future Proof Sales Strategy*

"The best sales professionals always help their customer solve real problems. *Buyer Centered Selling* is a necessary tool in helping sales teams serve their clients better. A powerful book loaded with the best ideas, strategies, and methods to create winning sales relationships. With detailed tactics, insightful questions, and relevant stories, this book enables you to help and serve in a truly collaborative way. A must read for true sales professionals."

**Mareo McCracken,**
Chief Revenue Officer, Movemedical

# BUYER-CENTERED SELLING

Rob

Hope you enjoy the book!

Best Wishes

Tom Witt

# BUYER-CENTERED SELLING

## HOW MODERN SELLERS ENGAGE & COLLABORATE WITH BUYERS

Thomas Williams & Thomas Saine

*Buyer-Centered Selling: How Modern Sellers Engage & Collaborate with Buyers*

For information about this title or to order other books and/or electronic media, contact the publisher:
Complex Sale Publishing
Thomas Williams
Thomas Saine
Strategic Dynamics Inc.
twilliams@strategicdynamicsfirm.com

978-1-948974-04-2 (hardcover)
978-1-948974-05-9 (softcover)
978-1-948974-06-6 (eBook)

Printed in the United States of America

Publisher's Cataloging-In-Publication Data
*(Prepared by The Donohue Group, Inc.)*

Names: Williams, Thomas (Thomas J.), 1949– author. | Saine, Thomas, author.

Title: Buyer-centered selling : how modern sellers engage & collaborate with buyers / Thomas Williams & Thomas Saine.

Description: [Scottsdale, Arizona] : Complex Sale Publishing, [2019] | Includes bibliographical references and index.

Identifiers: ISBN 9781948974042 (hardcover) | ISBN 9781948974059 (softcover) | ISBN 9781948974066 (ebook)

Subjects: LCSH: Selling. | Consumer behavior. | Industrial procurement.

Classification: LCC HF5438.25 .W55 2019 (print) | LCC HF5438.25 (ebook) | DDC 658.85--dc23

Rob

Check out chapters 1-5 and chapter 11. These might be most applicable to what your teaching.

Best to you.

Tom Witten

# PARADOX

611 OCEAN STREET SANTA CRUZ, CA 95060

# Table of Contents

# Dedication

This book is dedicated to Bob Miller, co-founder of Miller Heiman Inc.
Visionary, Author, Mentor and Friend

# Foreword

"There is no such thing as a new idea. It is impossible. We simply take a lot of old ideas and put them into a sort of mental kaleidoscope. We give them a turn and they make new and curious combinations. We keep on turning and making new combinations indefinitely; but they are the same old pieces of colored glass that have been in use through all the ages."

Mark Twain

While history's great inventors might have disagreed with Twain, there is a powerful message here for the sales profession, its contributors and critics. I'll come back to this shortly.

As a young man leaving the music profession, I felt rudderless. Playing music for a living was a fun ride for several years after music school. For a variety of reasons, it turned out to not be the right path for me.

Answering a job advertisement in *The Morning Call* newspaper, I soon found myself working in inbound sales for an entertainment agency of sorts that also sold imprinted advertising specialties.

Newsflash: I sucked at selling.

The owner saw something in me, though, and invested in me, training and coaching me, and teaching me his business. This was late 1984. While other methods did exist at the time, there was little in my world that was buyer centered. Customers had the money; my job was to get them to spend as much as possible with me. We used a memorized pitch that was as much carny barker as professional seller. We upsold, cross-sold, overcame objections with scripted snappy responses, and used the popular closing techniques of the time. And we did all this with assumptive confidence and a transfer of enthusiasm and positive energy.

The owner was a very intelligent, charismatic guy, who had systems and processes for running his small business, as he did for selling. I got good at it. It was a thrill. I found a new passion.

Around the time the passion kicked in, I started reading everything I could find about sales. I also came across the Nightingale-Conant company and bought cassette tape sets by Zig Ziglar, Brian Tracy, Denis Waitley, George Walther, Roger Dawson, Mike Wickett, and others. I listened in the car; I listened on my Sony Walkman®. I listened to some of these tape sets so much that I could talk along with them, practicing the author's inflection. I also found Tom Hopkins' two books, *How to Master the Art of Selling* and *The Official Guide to Success*. I became a subscriber to what was then *Personal Selling Power* (today, *Selling Power*). I started to record myself, both audio and video recordings—practicing, drilling, and rehearsing, like I had done in music, to become the best salesperson I could be.

With some success under my belt and my passion noticed, the owner started having me do outbound sales for the advertising side of the business. Since we had provided imprinted merchandize for a local Sears grand opening, I decided to chase Sears as a national client, calling on the marketing leader in the Sears tower in Chicago, from my little metal desk and folding chair in Allentown, PA. Using everything I learned and a dogged persistence that would have made my Dachshund proud, after nine months, I landed Sears—a national account that turned out to be the single largest customer for our business.

Fast forward a few years, and I'm in corporate America, working for a Fortune 100 company. Something happened there that completely changed the trajectory of my career. The first was some training in professional selling by the company. It was different. Less technique—more communication skill.

Secondly, through networking contacts at Toastmasters and my own continued exploration, I learned about other authors and a different approach to selling. Suddenly I was reading books from authors like Mack Hanan, Linda Richardson, Ron Willingham, Bob Miller, and Steve Heiman. One of my Toastmasters contacts was a salesperson for Dale Carnegie & Associates, and before long, I was a graduate of The Dale Carnegie Course and had become a graduate assistant.

Suddenly, things had shifted. Sales had moved from being mostly a bag of tricks to being something you did to help others. And in addition to the sales passion, I caught the training bug. The rest is history, and you can see that on LinkedIn or with an Internet search.

A few decades after my unexpected start in the sales profession, I'm honored to be writing this foreword for Tom Williams and Tom Saine.

Why am I honored?

Back to Mark Twain.

Look, there are no new ideas here. "The Toms," as I call them, have their own way of explaining things, their own terms, and their own graphics, acronyms, and models. But the concepts of buyer personas, exit criteria, deep discovery, joint solution design, or aligning the buying and selling processes and achieving sales success though a relentless pursuit of helping buyers solve their problems or enable their opportunities—these concepts aren't new.

THEY ARE JUST UNUSED BY MOST SALESPEOPLE IN MOST ORGANIZATIONS!

Crazy, right?

I'm fond of saying that "Life is a bell curve," so for clarity, I'm not saying there aren't any sales pros or organization doing these things or doing them well. I've conducted top-producer analysis for over sixteen years, and there are phenomenal sellers out there and every organization has its top producers. Great selling, however—especially at the level of Buyer-Centered Selling suggested in this book by Tom Williams and Tom Saine—is not pervasive today. Data from analysts like CSO Insights, vendors like the

Objective Management Group (OMG), or research publishers like Demand Gen Report, consistently supports this gap (and the need to close it). Tom Williams and Tom Saine have enriched our insight into the process of buyer-centered selling.

While many organizations achieve their annual revenue goals, only 50–60% of sales representatives make quota. According to OMG data, what they define as "weak salespeople" make up 50% of the sales population. While most organization leaders would say they are focused on their buyers and customers, B2B buyer research consistently tells us that many buyers are dissatisfied with seller behavior and do not trust sellers. We have much work to do to improve.

So, the power in this book—the seeds for greatness—isn't just the newness of the concepts and ideas that the authors share. It's powerful because it is an absolutely outstanding compilation of the best thinking on buyer-centered selling. It is what The Toms have seen produce excellent results, over their years in the business—having evolved over time, as I did in my earlier story—to their current place of enlightenment. (And yes, I use the term enlightenment purposefully.)

As Twain wrote, *"We simply take a lot of old ideas and put them into a sort of mental kaleidoscope. We give them a turn and they make new and curious combinations."* This is what I perceive The Toms have done. With the class, respect, and an other-oriented approach I have come to expect from them both, they have also included a ton of references to others' work—giving credit to those whose good work has influenced theirs.

However, in fairness to The Toms, and in recognition of their own thought leadership, I want to be clear that this is not *just* a regurgitation of others' work. Their own sales DNA is prevalent throughout this book. As lifelong learners themselves, they have curated, codified, tested, refined, evolved, shaped, and documented their Buyer-Centered Selling methods, and have now published them for the world to benefit. This book can be read cover-to-cover or used as a companion field guide written to help the seller forge a partnership that engages and guides the buyer. Like their first book, *The Seller's Challenge,* this book is a deep-dive resource that aids sellers in problem-solving barriers to a sale.

So, whether you are a young person, venturing into your first sales position without training or experience, or whether you're a graduate of a university with a sales degree program supported by the Sales Education Foundation, or whether you are a seasoned sales veteran who realizes that buyer behavior has evolved and it is time to make a total buyer-centered shift, there is something you can get from this book to grow as a seller. How much, is up to you. Absorb and apply it all, and it will supercharge your career or your sales organization. That is my highest and best hope for you. And it's why I'm honored to be here.

Read. Learn. Apply. Succeed. And let The Toms know what you think, what you did, and how it worked. They are sincerely good people and would love hearing from you.

Mike Kunkle
Vice President of Sales Enablement Services
SPA, Inc. and SPASIGMA
www.linkedin.com/in/mikekunkle

# Preface

## The Bad Habits of Good People

Much of our behavior is habitual. It doesn't matter whether the situation is work or recreational, public or private; we are influenced by our habits. Most habits are reinforced behaviors that we've associated with a reward, like praise from a parent. Habits may also be born out of the desire to avoid some sanction or imagined threat, like falling or being teased by a schoolmate.

Our guess is, the way you tie your running shoes today is the same way you tied them ten or twenty years ago. We're also guessing that no one has challenged the way you tie your shoes. Nobody has said, "Wait a minute. You're tying your shoes all wrong!" We'll also bet that you've never searched YouTube to validate your method or to discover a better solution. In fact, you may have some ancient memories of a parent helping you tie your shoes. When you combine those faded memories of a nurturing parent with the indisputable success of the method that has survived for decades, all the pieces are in place for habitual behavior.

So most of us go through life with a collection of habits that are unchallenged and unquestioned. Childhood is a period of testing behaviors and learning consequences. We develop routines and behave in habitual ways in order to simplify everyday decisions—the way you start your car, bathe, dress, comb your hair. Without habits and daily routines, our lives would be complex and time consuming.

Not all habits are childhood routines. We create habits for work—it's our way to minimize uncertainty and avoid unnecessary decisions. How we answer the phone is one example. We certainly don't hear our cell phone ring and then take out a pen and paper and make a list of what choices we want to consider in answering the call.

Talk to any professional athlete, and they will tell you they spend hours each week perfecting habits that benefit them in competition. They practice until no decisions are required. They perform required behaviors automatically.

In a recent interview, a wide receiver on the local NFL team was asked how he prepared himself to catch passes that were thrown to him over his head. He explained that it's his job to prepare for the unexpected and difficult situations that may arise. He explained that two or three times a week he would get one member of the coaching staff to lob balls over his head. He would stand with his back to the coach. He couldn't see the ball coming until it breached his peripheral vision.

Some doubters may question whether this exercise is of any real benefit. Well, during his career, this wide receiver has caught the second most passing yards of any player in the history of the NFL—second only to Jerry Rice. His name is Larry Fitzgerald. He is known for catching impossible passes… especially ones thrown over his head—balls he prepared for by consciously and deliberately developing a habit that would kick in when he needed it. He advocates preparing for the unexpected and difficult challenges.

## Conversations That Define Us

For those of us who make our livelihood by selling and managing sellers, we depend on our ability to handle difficult and unexpected situations— most of which involve conversations with stakeholders and influencers. In a professional career, how many conversations have we had with customers or prospects? A thousand? Five thousand? Whether it's in a meeting room, restaurant, exhibit booth, or over our cell phones, conversations can win us business or haunt our efforts to sleep at night.

Social scientists explain that conversations (and the accompanying activities) are the "building blocks" of every relationship. Very close relationships result when they survive difficult conversations and endure arguments; they can still convey intimacy and affection.

In the formative weeks of a relationship, a single disappointing conversation—perhaps one that raises questions about credibility or trust—can irreparably undermine any attempt at a long-term relationship. Relationships are like bank accounts. Positive, enjoyable, and beneficial conversations are our deposits into the account, while conversations fraught with arguments and conflict can completely liquidate the relationship account.

When a seller calls on a prospect for the first time, there is no balance to the account. A negative or unsatisfactory conversation can skew the relationship into debt. Researchers have discovered that only 9% of all sellers who get an initial call with a buying executive are granted a second call.

The question that arises for all of us is, *"If we want to conduct effective sales calls, what old habits are we going to exchange for new buyer-centered skills? Are we willing to develop new habits and truly become client ready?"*

In our years of working with sellers of all skill levels, there seem to be five clusters of skills and competencies that sellers need to hone: researching, socializing, solving, collaborating, and guiding.

Far too many sellers rely on habits instead of refined and well-practiced skills. Why? Building a skill is hard work, whereas a habit is comfortable, easy, and self-assuring. In the course of our lifetime, we may engage in a million or more conversations as we build relationships with family, friends, and co-workers. You seldom plan these informal and spontaneous conversations. But if you fail to plan and rehearse your conversational skills with buying executives, you may become one of the 91% who fail to get a second conversation.

Too many sellers have the ingrained habit of talking about their product, its history and development, its capabilities and features. None of these topics may be of interest to a buying executive who is concerned about solving a problem that you have ignored or overlooked.

So, what are the conversational skills that can make us winners in building and enriching relationships in a buy-sell world? There are five skills or competencies.

- *Research.* In a world of social media and various platforms for accessing content, research is a vital skill that lies at the fulcrum of all other skills. Strong research skills can help guide you through the darkest times of a sale. Research helps you understand your buyer, the buyer's company, industry, and competitive landscape. Good researchers become "voices" and "experts" through chat rooms, videos, podcasts, blogs, and white papers. Strong research skills open your eyes to your buyer's world. Research enriches conversations and eases the flow of discussion.

- *Socialize.* In fact, the ability to socialize is often a strength of many sellers. They focus on relationship building and the communication techniques required to engage and connect—like sharing personal experiences, inquiring about the customer's hobbies or family, and kindling an emotional connection.

- *Solve.* Sellers need to sharpen their *solving* skills—their ability to help the buyer detect problems, opportunities, or threats, and grasp available solutions. Often this involves an ability to conduct "brand agnostic" conversations about problems the buyer has overlooked.

- *Collaborate.* Effective buyer-centered sellers have strong skills in *collaboration.* Becoming collaborative means cultivating the ability to work together—plan, share resources, and recognize common ground. Collaboration is far less accommodation than it is co-creation. Collaboration has its roots in trust and credibility, in transparency and a willingness to share risk.

- *Guide.* Last, a conversation skill often lacking in the seller's toolbox is *guidance.* Too many sellers mistake guidance for "pushing" their product. For buyer-centered sellers, providing guidance means developing a proven road map that shortens and simplifies the buying process, advocating one set of capabilities over a lesser set, and clearly outlining the next step in the process. Sometimes buyers get lost in the complexity and chaos of their own process.

Only with these skills can sellers become truly "customer ready." These skills define who you are and how you differ from your competitors. A buying executive once said, "If you want to know what matters to me most, teach me something I need to know about my customer. *Sellers need to understand their customer's customer.*"

## Exchanging Bad Habits for Key Competencies

This book was written for sellers and sales managers who are faced with complex B2B opportunities that seem to shift, evolve, and morph without warning. Just as you gain a clear lens into what the buyers want, the buying "context" changes. So how do you gain clarity into what they want and how do you measure their desired benefit? Relying on old, habitual reactions may be comfortable, but it may not be helpful.

One answer—an answer that we advocate—is for sellers to become more buyer focused in their selling strategy. They need to discover how to help their buyer simplify, organize, and manage the craziness of running a buying process. Help them problem solve, evaluate options, collaborate, and map a direction for change.

While you're reading this book, we recommend that you take a close examination of your sales related habits and skills. Where do you need to improve so that you can excel? Which habits need to be replaced by a professional skill or competency? At the end of each chapter, we suggest you identify a couple of habits that need to be repaired or replaced. Get a clear vision in your mind of what great conversation skills would do for your calls, meetings, and presentations.

In 2018 we co-authored *The Seller's Challenge: How Top Performers Master 10 Deal Killing Obstacles in B2B Sales*. Our motive in writing that book was to provide sellers with a "field manual" for assembling both tactics and strategies that address these specific deal killers. Our feedback on the book has been gratifying: it fits into a niche that sellers and sales managers want.

*Buyer-Centered Selling: How Top Sellers Engage & Collaborate with Buyers* combines "seller's challenges" with "buyer's dilemmas." We recognized from our discussions with buyers, committees, and corporate executives that every sales opportunity is two-sided: it presents challenges and obstacles for both buyer and seller. Many B2B purchasing decisions are driven by complex, high priced products and services that provide the foundation for powerful revenue streams. Without the collaborative efforts of both seller and buyer, many buying processes are doomed by lethargy, fear, and eroding internal support from the buying community.

So how can we knit together these two communities into joint commitments that serve the interests of both? Perhaps we need a different approach to selling—one built on collaboration. This isn't new or earthshaking. It does require a broader skill set that includes research, socializing, problem solving, collaboration, and guidance.

*Buyer-Centered Selling* provides strategies and tactics to help the buyer address eleven dilemmas likely to slow and obstruct the buying process. The reader will discover quickly that buying and selling are inextricably connected.

Each chapter is independent but unified by a common commitment to help the customer buy.

In Chapter 1, *Footprints of Change: The Challenges of Buyer-Centered Selling,* we focus on how buying and selling are changing, the emergence of the "digital native," and why you should consider a different approach to engaging the buyer, an approach we refer to as "buyer-centered selling."

Chapter 2, *Get Connected: Adapt to the Customer's Buying Process,* explores how to map a buying process and align buying and selling activities that expedite a decision. Buyer-centered sellers want to provide buyers what they need, when they need it.

Chapter 3, *The Tortoise and the Hare: How to Win with Buyer-Centered Discovery,* shares how an effective sales discovery process can bring buyer and seller together through a shared focus on problems, implications, and solutions.

*From Jekyll to Hyde: Selling to a Buyer's Behavioral Style,* Chapter 4, is a journey through four behavioral styles and how buyer-centered sellers can adjust and adapt to how the customer wishes to receive and process information.

In Chapter 5, *Differentiating with Value Messages that Snap, Crackle and Pop!* we explore how to use your communication plan to differentiate your product and yourself.

Chapter 6, *Jewels from the Junk Yard: Resuscitating Stalled Opportunities,* reminds us that stalled opportunities may be "jewels" that require a little nurturing and encouragement to become a vital addition to your pipeline or funnel.

Chapter 7, *Scared Straight: Selling to Risk Averse Buyers,* takes a close look at an issue that troubles many of us—a buyer's perception of risk and their fear of failure.

In Chapter 8, *Cold Case Files: Activating Dormant Leads and Inactive Accounts,* we're reminded that dormant leads and inactive accounts represent excellent prospecting targets.

*Unlocking the Executive Mindset: Selling Up,* Chapter 9, focuses on how research can help unlock an executive's mindset, enrich sales calls, and become the "ideal seller."

Chapter 10, *Is Your Cross-Selling Program Driving You Crazy?* For many of us, cross selling can be a boon to our selling effort or a real waste of our time. In this chapter we explore myths, obstacles, and best approaches to expanding your footprint in your target organization

In Chapter 11, *Secrets to Closing Like a Pro!* we provide a collection of valuable tactics for finalizing a deal. We explore the core elements to a close, barriers to closing a deal, and secrets for managing a successful close.

## This Book Is Written for:

**Frontline Sales Professionals:** You are the revenue generators for your company. This book is written to address obstacles, barriers, and challenges that you have shared with us.

**Sales Leadership:** You ensure the growth, discipline, and skill sets needed for your company's health and survival. Your sales representatives need your insight, guidance, and support.

**Learning & Development Directors:** We have blended thought leadership, concept acquisition, and skill development into our book, companion workbook, concept cards, programs, and workshops.

**Sales Enablement Executives:** You want measurable results, improvements, and commitment to change. We are available to support and guide the integration of the book's content into an exciting format for change.

**Account Managers:** You manage the day-to-day interface of the customer with your organization and you cross-sell additional products and services. You're a therapist, magician, politician and physician.

**Marketing Professionals:** You develop sales ready leads and help foster retention and referrals. You assist the sales organization by creating sales content that provides insights and differentiation.

**Service Personnel:** You sell preventative maintenance and service contracts and you are often the first line of defense when repairs or upgrades are required. In your unique role you are often the eyes and ears of the organization monitoring satisfaction and loyalty levels post sale.

**CEOs:** Ultimatelly you're responsible for the number and there is no bottom line until there is a top line.

Whatever your win-loss ratio, your quota, or your close rate, recognize that the world of B2B sales is changing. The old "tried and true" behaviors may no longer carry you to the winner's circle. Invest in yourself. Sell smart!

Tom Williams

Tom Saine

# Chapter 1

# The Footprints of Change: The Challenges of Buyer-Centered Selling

"The world around us is shifting—in virtually every way. Savvy sellers have caught on to the fact that B2B buying behavior is changing as well."

Ago Cluytens—Contributor to *Rain Today*

In today's business world, the only constant is change. Disruptive innovations and technology are creating new products, new delivery channels, and new ways for buyers and sellers to interact. What does this mean? Buyers are faced with more choices and greater complexity than ever. For the seller, we must anticipate and embrace change and provide our buyers with a seamless customer experience.

## The Footprints of Change

During the the last decade, authors have written extensively about the 3rd Platform (more formally, the third industrial revolution) and how it has held us in its grip. The 3rd Platform underscores massive changes in technology, including the emergence of Cloud Computing, Big Data (now "analytics"), Mobility (portable communication), and Social Media.[1]

What does this mean for those of us in the sales profession? There is more information available, distributed on more platforms to more people more quickly than ever before. This means that there are more data available on new product pipelines, client experiences, test results, and competitors. Buying organizations have staff with greater product knowledge and business acumen. The result is greater complexity in the buying process and stakeholders with more fully developed preferences and opinions and little time to devote to sellers.

As one author explains, "The role customers and sellers play has changed. B2B customers have access to more information, have to gain more buy-in internally, and have a growing number of options to evaluate."[2] This transformation presents new challenges for both buyer and seller.

On the buyer's side, purchasing committees continue to increase in size, making buying more complex and resource intensive. Each additional stakeholder increases the length of time it takes to reach a decision and the likelihood of a stalled buying process. Consider what an increase in the number of stakeholders does to the deliberation process in making a purchase—more critics, more questions to be answered, and greater diversity of opinion on value and price. Then there is the difficulty in scheduling meetings, sharing knowledge, and evaluating options. With growing complexity, there is the ever-increasing prospect of a failed buying process. Buyers are desperate to simplify and speed the process without compromising their primary objective: purchase a quality, affordable, risk-free product, service, or solution.

Toman, Adamson, and Gomez observe that "with a wealth of data on any solution, a raft of stakeholders involved in each purchase, and an ever-expanding array of options, more and more deals bog down or even halt altogether. Customers are increasingly overwhelmed and often more paralyzed than empowered."[3]

On the seller's side, we are challenged to collaborate with buyers who are increasingly isolated and restrictive in their struggle to overcome forces that commoditize our products and services. As the number of stakeholders increases, we wrestle with how best to allocate time and corporate resources to avoid stalled and lengthy buying processes.

There is more change ahead. Soon we'll be buffeted by the headwinds and tailwinds of a new and powerful industrial revolution driven by artificial intelligence and digital applications with billions of users.[4] As sales professionals, we can be either victims of change or the managers of change. We must choose: either allow our customers to struggle and often falter, or provide them the guidance and direction they need.

Individuals, families, businesses, and even towns have failed in the wake of change.

### Story: The Corridors of Change

There are many examples of famous market-leading companies that have fallen to bankruptcy as a result of misreading the signposts and market indicators of change. In 1896, the Dow Jones Industrial Index comprised twelve companies: American Cotton Oil, American Sugar, American Tobacco, Chicago Gas, Distilling and Cattle Feeding, General Electric, Laclede Gas, National Lead, North American, Tennessee Coal and Iron, U.S. Leather Preferred, and U.S. Rubber. Only General Electric has survived.

In the late 1880s Bodie, California, had more than 10,000 residents, 2,000 buildings, 200 restaurants, and 65 bars. Now it's a quiet cluster of abandoned buildings with an occasional national historic marker. At its height, the discovery of gold fueled Bodie's constellation of businesses.

Talk to the residents of Bruceton, Tennessee, about change. Once a manufacturing hub for the region, businesses began laying off workers in 1996 as the result of the NAFTA agreement. The Henry I. Seigel Company once employed more than 1,700 workers but closed its doors in 2000.

In recent years, we have seen Polaroid, Blockbuster, Napster, ToysRus, Kodak, Blackberry, Borders Bookstore, Circuit City, CompUSA, Atari, and Enron fail.

They have been replaced by new enterprises in new markets. Think Spotify, Instagram, Square, Whatsapp, Uber, Airbnb, PayPal, and Oculus.

While these names have become a part of our business vocabulary, none of these companies were in business before 2008. Also, none manufacture anything. Each impacts how we conduct our daily lives by changing how buyers buy.

Change always leaves a footprint.

---

## The Challenge of Buyer-Centered Selling

***The Buyer's Dilemma:* Buyers are struggling to simplify and speed the buying process without compromising their primary objective: purchase a quality, affordable, risk-free product, service, or solution.** Buyers have more choices, are better informed, and are more demanding of a frictionless customer experience. But they are plagued with complexity and the changing dynamics of their internal processes.

***The Seller's Challenge:* Sellers are wrestling with how to restore life to stalled or derailed buying processes, differentiate their product in an increasingly commoditized market, and help the buying organization develop an appetite and sense of urgency for change.** The seller's role in the buying process is a new and challenging one: collaborate with buyers to share insight, craft a buying road map, provide guidance, unify stakeholders behind a common course of action, and make the buying organization "change ready."

---

In this chapter, we'll explore the changing world of B2B from both a buyer's and seller's perspective, the concept of buyer-centered selling, and how we can work collaboratively to guide and simplify the challenges facing our customer.

## THE TRANSFORMATIONAL IMPACT OF TECHNOLOGY ON B2B SALES

So how will this acceleration of technology challenge those of us who buy and sell? Consider the following nine implications of technological change.[5]

1. **Mobility is enabling sellers and buyers to interact anytime and anywhere.** Buying is soon to become an "anywhere, anytime" process as buyers access valuable data and proof points in real time.

2. **Data is becoming the key to driving greater productivity.** Imagine a work environment where products and people are tracked by sensors. Product sensors will automatically gauge inventories, plan deliveries to customers and evaluate the aging of products. Artificial intelligence (AI) will become an integral part of every change process.

3. **CRM systems and sales analytics will drive engagements.** CRM systems will become the seller's navigational system, dictating who, how, and why we communicate. Sales analytics will benchmark our progress and success.

4. **Artificial intelligence is beginning to guide and advise sellers.** CRM systems will highlight the highest probability actions in a buying process. Sales executives will rely on CRM systems for predictive models, customer sentiment and experience, skill development, and gap assessments.

5. **Virtual reality (VR) is augmenting purchasing.** VR devices will guide customers through virtual stores. While seated at their desk, the customer will place an order, and the automated fulfillment system will complete the order and delivery process.

6. **Customization is driving purchasing decisions.** Customers expect seamless integration of new products with existing business operations. "Off-the-shelf" or "one size fits all" products are suspect to the savvy buyer.

7. **Elements of the buying process are becoming automated.** Sensors and machines will interact to fortify and speed data-driven decisions. Where applicable, contracts, especially for reorders, will be automated.

8. **Machine learning and sensors are driving statistical modeling.** Predictive models will tell business leaders where to look for revenue streams and where to abandon hope.

9. **Customers have a heightened expectation for quality service.** This creates a desire for deeper and richer service-based relationships between buyer and seller. Transactional selling jobs such as telemarketing or the sale of highly commoditized products will continue to become automated.

The implication of extensive technological change is that it places a greater burden on sellers to understand how change is impacting the buyer, the buyer's customer, and the buyer's industry.

### The Rise of the "Digital Native"

Quickly, a new dynamic is beginning to redefine the direction for B2B purchasing—the rise of the digital native. "Digital natives who grew up with the internet and smartphone have transformed the way B2B buyers research purchases, qualify vendors, and make purchases—changing the rules of the game for marketers and product managers."[6]

While it seems that all aspects of our physical world are touched by the power of technology, there are other economic, demographic, and geo-political factors in play. Many of these forces challenge traditional perspectives on buying and selling. Digital natives are relying more on process automation, easy access to product and vendor information, and quick responses from their network and members of their digital community. In short, buyers are compressing the purchasing process by minimizing the role of sellers.

What are the "signposts" of change for those of us who buy and sell?

1. Digital natives are driving change as both consumers and the dominant demographic in the world of B2B buying.

2. Procurement departments have grown in size, authority, and expertise. Many Procurement teams now report directly to a member of the executive team.

3. Increased commoditization is undermining the marketing of value while marginalizing differences that distinguish good options from great decisions. .

4. Globalization is opening new markets and challenging traditional avenues of growth.

5. Consolidation is a powerful force redefining leadership in many sectors.

6. Transactional selling jobs are being automated.

7. Customization is driving many purchasing decisions.

8. CRM systems and sales analytics are beginning to drive engagements.

Stop for a moment and answer this question: who suffers most from the turmoil created by change? While it's easy to feel sorry for the seller, it's the buyer who bears the responsibility for planning, adapting to, and implementing change. As sellers and sales executives, we are challenged to execute sales activities that enable buyers to buy. This means we must help the buyer follow a course of action that simplifies the buying process.

## THE MODERN B2B BUYER

Faced with a daunting backlog of requests, buyers are compressing the buying process by complementing vendor scorecards and product assessments with social media, third-party web sites, and input from colleagues in a similar industry. To better understand the changing dynamics of B2B buying, consider the following trends among modern buyers.

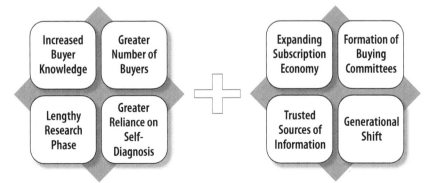

Figure 1-1: Trends Facing Modern Sellers

1. **Increased Buyer Knowledge:** Buyers are more informed than ever before due to the volume of content and speed with which information can be accessed.[7] Today's buyer searches Google first; then they read articles and blogs, watch videos, and download whitepapers.[8] They review prospective supplier websites and download product literature, eBooks, and other content. "74% of buyers choose the sales representative that was first to add value and insight."[9] The challenge facing buyers, especially those managing the buying process, is to ensure that all stakeholders are exposed to the right content at the right point in the buyer's journey.

   Educating the buyer has become a significant challenge. Sellers are engaging buyers who have extensive product sophistication. "Prospects are self-educating at an accelerating rate."[10] It's vital that sellers upgrade and retool their sales call skills when working with well-informed buyers.

2. **Greater Number of Buyers:** Gartner reports that, on average, 7 stakeholders contribute to each purchase, which is up from 5.4 year over year.[11] The implication for buyers is the need to deploy and manage a buying process that is more complex than in the past and burdened by stakeholders with divergent expectations.

   As the number of buyers increases, the buying cycle becomes more complex, requiring a greater investment of sales time to access all stakeholders involved. The resulting divergence in personal and organizational priorities makes it difficult for buying groups to agree to anything more than "to move cautiously" "avoid risk," and "save money."[12] The challenge for the seller is to bring unity to a chorus of different voices singing in a different key.

3. **Lengthy Research Phase:** "The 2016 B2B Buyer's Survey Report shows that buyers continue to carefully and thoroughly research potential purchases, with almost half of those surveyed stating that their purchase cycle is longer than the prior year."[13] 70.25% of buyers

wait until after they have fully defined needs before they engage a sales professional, and 44.25% identify needs first.[14] It is not uncommon for a buyer to short-list several suppliers for further discussion. As a result of their research, buyers often determine they have a problem, opportunity, or threat, and they explore potential solutions before they even engage with a seller. In *The Challenger Sale,* the authors note that 57% of the modern buyer's decision process is completed prior to engaging sellers.

4.  **Greater Reliance on Self-Diagnosis:** Buyers often conduct a thorough vetting process that is a disadvantage to smaller, newer, and less publicized companies. 75% of B2B buyers now use social media to qualify suppliers.[15] These "house run" qualifying processes work to the advantage of market leaders with extensive client lists and a broad social media presence.

    The result is that sellers are faced with a longer sales cycle, a later "entry point" into that sales cycle, and later access to influential buyers.

5.  **Expanding Subscription Economy:** The world is moving from products to services. Subscriptions are exploding because millions of digital customers are favoring access over ownership.[16] Think Netflix and Amazon Prime.

    Buyers also often request multiple, flexible financial proposals that minimize capital expenditures. For too long, Executive Buyers—those who are responsible for the project and have funding authority for the purchase—have been burdened by expensive technology that has often been "more than they need."

6.  **Formation of Buying Committees.** Increasingly, buyers are forming buying groups, buying centers, or buying committees within their organization, and they are requiring a consensus on what product, service, or solution should be purchased. A joint decision-making process gives the group leverage in co-creating value and negotiating prices and terms that reduce their purchase risk.

Buying committees pose unique challenges for sellers. While most are dedicated to getting the best product for the lowest price, many use scorecards that overvalue price. Successful sellers are quick to develop internal sponsors, discover stakeholders that manage the decision process, and uncover how members rate products.

7. **Trusted Sources of Information:** HubSpot reports that 30% of buyers speak with peers when they are ready to buy.[17] In 2017, the most trusted sources of information were word-of-mouth, customer references/case studies, media articles, vendor-authored materials, analyst reports, crowdsourced reviews, and the salesperson.[18]

   76% of buyers factor in a timely response from sellers when deciding which product to purchase.[19] 74% of buyers choose to buy a product from the first seller that adds value and insight.[20]

8. **Generational Shift.** According to Forrester, by 2025 millennials will form 44% of the U.S. workforce. Furthermore, 73% of millennials are involved in B2B purchasing decisions.[21] This means sellers must adapt to a generation that is driven to use technology and social media to collaborate along with the phone and email. This means the new buyer is hyper connected and socially influenced.

## WHO DOES YOUR BUYER WANT YOU TO BE?

Several years ago, we conducted a unique "ice breaker" for one of our programs. It was more by accident than design, and we got much more than we anticipated.

We asked the thirty participants in the workshop to write a two- or three-word description of what they do for their customers that is impactful and insert it below their name on their place cards. The "catch" was the participant couldn't use the words "seller" or "sales" in the description. It was meant to be a job title from their customer's perspective.

To give them an example, we told the story of a sales vice president who defines his job as an "executive therapist." He explains that he helps executives discover what troubles them, and then he creates an action plan to mitigate their anxieties and concerns.

The result was disappointing. We harvested a crop of dead and dying expressions: "master deal-maker," "preferred supplier," "brand representative," "senior account executive," and "corporate liaison" to name a few.

The purpose of the exercise was to bring to the surface how sellers present themselves to their prospects and customers. However, it unlocked a more vital issue of the alignment between how sellers present themselves and the role our prospects want us to provide. *Are we who our customers want us to be?*

A few weeks later we turned to a focus group of buyers who shared a very different story. We heard the following remarks:

"Our world is changing so rapidly, we need someone who's on our team—someone who can help us overcome our internal obstacles to change."

"We need a sales representative who has been through this before and understands how to shepherd a committee to meet timelines and commitments."

"I don't want a faithful follower—I want a leader. I want someone who is blatantly truthful and able to coach us across the finish line. If that doesn't work, then I want him to drag us across."

One of the most revealing comments was simple and eloquent. "I want someone whose desire to get it done is as great as mine. Everything else is just a promise."

As we reflected on our notes and the comments from the group of buyers, several conclusions became clear. First, some buying processes have become so complex that post-sale implementation can undermine the purchase. Second, executive leadership monitors these decision processes closely. We better prepare to make each opportunity an operational success. Third, executive level sponsors see purchasing decisions as "stepping stones" toward the successful execution of vital corporate initiatives. Fourth, buyers see sellers as solution architects, not as product purveyors.

Many research groups have conducted surveys, interviews, polls, and focus groups to uncover what is lacking in their conversations with sellers.

The following are common expectations executives raise about the roles of sellers.

- "All I expect is a collaborative discussion among peers focused on proven solutions from similar industries."
- "A seller who understands our business model and can capture how we need to connect and serve our customers."
- "A road map for moving forward in integrating technology."
- "Someone who is knowledgeable of market trends and barriers to change."
- "Someone who knows how to prioritize and integrate emerging technologies that will drive growth."
- "Someone who will take the time to understand where we are going."
- "Someone who knows how to embrace Artificial Intelligence while taking a responsible approach to capital expenditures."
- "A sales representative who understands how to apply data analytics to their product and affiliated production processes."
- "Someone who can help us anticipate and predict threats before they surface."

One executive offered a metaphor that seems to capture the situation that many buyers are facing. " I feel like a patient in a hospital. After becoming acquainted with the various diagnostic equipment, I'm expected to diagnose and treat my own illness."

## WHAT IS BUYER-CENTERED SELLING?

> Becoming buyer-centered is both a mindset and strategy focused on helping prospective buyers improve their current state through collaborative action.

During rapid technological change, shifts in demographics, economics, geography, and political agendas, we are challenged with helping our buyers navigate business obstacles that threaten their interest in buying. Becoming buyer-centered is both a mindset and strategy focused on helping prospective buyers improve their current state through collaborative action. The essential burden in becoming buyer-centered is a heavy one: help the buying organization become "change ready."

Buyer-centered selling is not a methodology, a step-by-step process, or a theory of sales. Instead, it is a philosophy about the seller's responsibility for building relationships, delivering on promises, and aiding buyers. It's about becoming a valued consultant, a change specialist, or a team member—depending on the skill set and advice your buyer needs. It's about solving problems, predicting threats, and helping clients capitalize on revenue generating opportunities. It's about a philosophy grounded in collaboration, education, and transparency. It is a "buyer first" perspective. It is about how to educate, nurture, and solve. How you sell now becomes a key differentiator.

There is an often-told story about the great sales evangelist Zig Zigler. A man came up to him after a presentation and said, "I've read your books and listened to your presentations. Nothing I do helps me sell better. What should I do?" Zigler answered, "Stop selling, and go help someone."

Buyer-centered selling is not new or revolutionary. Its origin lies with many sales authors, scholars, and evangelists. The only novelty is that the seller brings new tools, advice, and skills while building bridges individual by individual and department by department. What is your buyer's need?

Some buyers need help building unified support when obstacles surface. Other buyers need leadership in mitigating risk, tracking timelines, and using new technologies.

So, if buyer-centered selling is a philosophy grounded in helping our buyers and stakeholders, what benefits do we bring to the buying process?

## Eight Core Elements of Buyer-Centered Selling

Consider these eight key "deliverables" that we owe the buyer as a partner and ally.

Figure 1-2: Eight Core Elements of Buyer-Centered Selling

1. **Insights that Educate:** Insights get stakeholders to think differently. "Insights can drive a buyer to reconsider their perspective on a problem, opportunity, or a threat."[22] Insights can take the form of stories, events, or testimonials that prompt an emotional connection with the stakeholder. These are vital tools for sellers who are selling against the status quo or creating differentiation. Insights have the added impact of:
   - Piquing a buyer's interest in discussing a new way to think about or improve their business. This requires research.
   - Building credibility with the buyer
   - Broadening the buyer's awareness through education
   - Getting the buyer and seller "on the same page"
   - Pressing a buyer's emotional levers, such as fear, pride, excitement.

2. **Map & Align Buy-Sell:** Mapping a succinct and appropriate buying process can position the buyer to expedite what otherwise might become a complex and overwhelming project. Alignment connects sales activities to the appropriate phases of the buyer's journey by expanding their choices and enriching their decision-making. Give buyers the help they need when they need it.[23] It's the seller's job to make buying easier. Alignment helps:
   - Determine which selling activities are needed to expedite the buying process

- Recognize stakeholders who are at different stages and address their needs
- Predict and understand the causes of a stalled buying process

3. **Prescriptive Guidance:** The seller offers direction that drives disaffection with the present state or status quo. While accommodative, the seller is an advocate for change—an "activist." The seller's responsibility is to:
   - Demonstrate a knowledge of business and finance, i.e., business acumen
   - Offer a pathway or road map that helps the buyer and the buyer's organization become "change ready"
   - Show that the cost of inaction is painful and far exceeds the cost of change. Sellers must be comfortable with a financial discussion.
   - Create disaffection with the status quo and provide an outcome that's better than the current state

4. **Discovery Process:** Sales discovery provides stakeholders with the opportunity to voice their concerns, expectations, and desires. Sellers accomplish this with excellent questioning and listening skills asked in a non-offensive manner. Consider this example. "Your production defect rate for faulty products is 7%, and the corporate objective is to reduce the rate to 3% within the next year. What steps do you need to take in order to meet the corporate mandate?" An effective discovery process helps:
   - Bring a problem-solving focus to executive level conversations
   - Identify the gap. This is "the place between the current state and the future state. The gap is where the value of the sale lives."[24]
   - Provide a valuable opportunity for the seller to detect each stakeholder's concerns
   - Portray the seller as a mapmaker and consultant for the buying process

- Discovery is not a singular event. It occurs throughout the entire buy-sell process.

5. **Dynamic Value Messaging:** When sellers adopt a strategy of dynamic value messaging, they are able to convey value in a form (or currency) that matters to each stakeholder. The common denominator for all stakeholders is productivity.[25] The outcome of dynamic value messaging is to:
   - Build a common ground among all stakeholders
   - Create differentiation by connecting to what matters most to each stakeholder.

6. **Consensus Building:** Often buyers are faced with stakeholders who have divergent views. The buyer-centered seller acts as a consensus builder to unify buyers who hold disparate opinions or have reached conflicting conclusions. Consensus building helps:
   - Share information and provide reassurances that unify stakeholders and minimize differences
   - Avoid stalled decision processes by creating a unified group position.

7. **Risk Mitigation:** Fear of risk associated with change can stall or undermine a buying process. Buyer-centered sellers anticipate fears and act to minimize perceived risk. Everyone expects some level of risk. But each stakeholder has a different capacity for fear. Which fears are annoying? Which fears are paralyzing? An effective risk mitigation plan helps:
   - Quell stakeholder fears associated with change
   - Minimize perceived risk by providing documentation, testimonials, and case studies from similar industries that reduce feelings of uncertainty
   - Convey the cost of inaction and threat that arises from indecision

8. **Social Presence:** Social media is the pathway to community discussions that interest your buyers. It gives sellers the opportunity to "listen" to buyers, and it provides buyers with the opportunity to gauge who has knowledge and experience that may prove valuable in achieving high priority corporate initiatives. While the benefits of social presence are numerous, the effective use of social media helps:

   - Build credibility and name recognition that can assist prospecting and qualifying
   - Provide insight that may increase a buyer's receptivity to selling activity
   - Create a sense of comfort and confidence in purchasing your product

## The Five Commitments of Collaboration

Buyer-centered selling doesn't happen without the coordination of a buyer and seller. It takes candor, trust, and a healthy dose of transparency from both parties. Buyer and seller must discuss and reach an agreement on five issues that will help the two achieve a common focus for planning and action.

Figure 1-3: The Five Commitments of Collaboration

1. **Commitment: Define Goal & Direction**—*What does the buyer want to correct, avoid, or achieve?*
   - Understand the challenge (problem, threat, or opportunity) through the buyer's eyes
   - Capture what is at stake for the buyer and company

- Assess the urgency to act
- Evaluate the capacity of the current provider to overcome their current state

2. **Commitment: Probe Cause & Effect**—*What factors lie at the root of today's current state?*
   - Determine the origin, or root cause, and contributing factors
   - Assess attempts to correct the current state that failed
   - Gauge the support for change among stakeholders

3. **Commitment: Gauge Obstacles to Change**—*How can we uncover and address obstacles that may stall or stop plans to change?*
   - Assess internal support for change
   - Clarify political and procedural dynamics that may create barriers to change
   - Understand buyer preferences

4. **Commitment: Identify Measurable Outcomes**—*What outcomes must the desired solution produce?*
   - Understand the buyer's desired business outcomes and any gap that exists and its cause
   - Determine benchmarks on a timeline

5. **Commitment: Jointly Plan Action**—*How can we coordinate our efforts and collaborate on a pathway to a solution?*
   - Reach agreement with all key buyers on the best course of action
   - Identify necessary information and resources
   - Establish timelines

## Obstacles to a Buyer-Centered Approach

We've all faced prospects who treated sellers as opponents and viewed the buying process as a contest among gladiators. It would be foolish and self-defeating to believe that all buyers are open to collaboration. In fact, many buyers—including some purchasing agents and procurement executives—believe the best deals are struck from fierce competition between buyer and seller. While many of these buyers exist there are others that want a fair deal with a reliable supplier that fulfills their promises.

However, there are signposts that suggest a buyer-centered approach may not be a good fit—at least, not immediately and not without some effort.

Let's consider five warning signs. When reflected in the buyer's behavior, they suggest a buyer-centered approach may be problematic.

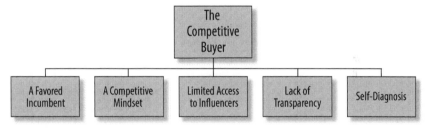

Figure 1-4: Five Warning Signs of a Competitive Buyer

1. **A Favored Incumbent.** On occasion, a buyer will have a preferred supplier, but to the outside seller, there is no clear evidence that the current supplier is favored. Here are some questions to ask yourself. Is the buyer unwilling to admit to a problem, threat, or opportunity underlying the buying process? Does the buyer seem resistant or reluctant to answer questions surrounding change? (Example, "How does your team feel about change?") Is the buyer hesitant to accept assistance, information, white papers, or blogs that are "brand agnostic"?

2. **A Competitive Mindset.** A buyer's mindset can be hard to read. Often, it's masked by moods, defensive responses, accusations, and time pressure. But a competitive mindset can stand out like a bullhorn in a cemetery. Competitive buyers can be curt, prideful, self-possessed, and egotistical (just like some sellers). Some competitive buyers will challenge the seller on the smallest of issues and make accusations that are intended to rile and upset the seller. These buyers look at all aspects of a sale as "win or lose" battles. Their competitive mindset results from a combination of personality and how they see

their role in the organization. As with the rest of us, it's difficult to change behavioral styles that have been ingrained and reinforced over the years. Almost anyone who has experience working with a buyer who has a competitive mindset can tell the uninitiated seller what they should expect. But there are ways to overcome a competitive mindset. A seller can offer assistance on a small but valuable task. (Example: Suppose you just read a newly released research report by Forrester. Their work is highly credible and "brand agnostic." Offer to send the buyer a copy.)

3. **Limited Access to Influencers.** When sellers are limited in their access to stakeholders, this is a big red flag. While restricting the seller's ability to understand needs, identify priorities, and gauge interest in change, a lack of access undermines efforts to collaborate or assist the buying process. A seller's discovery process withers quickly without the nourishment of contact. Highly restricted access is a clear "no go" for a buyer-centered sales strategy.

4. **Lack of Transparency.** Sellers should consider the information available to them on their CRM. Not much there? Without access to influencers and transparency, it's difficult to develop and execute a sales strategy. Even if the seller is given access to influencers, if influencers are unwilling to share concerns, change is a long shot.

5. **Self-Diagnosis.** We've all had customers who assessed their current state, analyzed their concerns, and are now ready to buy. "Just give me a price." But what if they misdiagnosed their problem or it's scope and size? There was no discovery process and no interviews with stakeholders to determine their preferences and priorities. It's similar to a physician handing her patient a signed (but blank) prescription. Buyers deserve due diligence even if it is foreshortened. What the buyer is really saying is "I want to shorten this process and get a solution in place (even if I don't know what the problem is)." What they need is

a consultant who can provide reliable insight, point the buyer in the right direction, and simplify the decision process.

## The Velvet Glove of Consulting

Earlier in this chapter, we raised an important question, "Who does your buyer want you to be?" A partial answer is they want or need a professional with industry knowledge, a clear focus on the buyer's needs, and the problem-solving skills of a consultant. They want a mapmaker who knows the shortcuts. This could be you. Some of the challenges outlined in this chapter require the velvet glove of consulting. How do you help people who are unsure they need or want help? How do you simplify choices when the options seem overwhelming? How do you glean vital bits of information from a raft of articles, test results, books, and marketing information? How can I simplify a job that seems fraught with complexity and risk?

Buyers are looking for prescriptive guidance. Following a Gartner/CEB study, researchers reported that "a proactive, prescriptive approach increases purchase ease by 86%. Prescriptive suppliers give a clear recommendation for action backed by a specific rationale; they present a concise offering and a stable view of their capabilities; they explain complex aspects of the purchase process clearly."[26]

These are the keys to keep in mind as you take a fresh look at your customer and grasp their needs. A prescriptive approach might include some or all of the following:

- Offer a simplified road map to a buying decision
- Cut out the frills and minimize due diligence
- Help the customer minimize options; "less is more"
- Establish benchmarks and timelines
- Translate value into your customer's terms
- Offer early solutions to risks, real or imaginary
- Help drive consensus; deal with pockets of dissent
- Hold brand-agnostic briefings with your customer

- Detect and neutralize potential barriers and obstacles
- Help your customer calculate the cost of inaction

In 1964 Bob Dylan wrote a song entitled "The Times They-Are-a-Changing." Today, the song could be re-released as a metaphor for the change that is occurring in the dynamic relationship between buyer and seller. Sellers today must adapt to a modern buyer who is challenged by a milieu that is complex and resource intensive. It's time to reconsider our approach and revitalize our skill set.

## Key Points to Remember for Buyer-Centered Selling
Consider the following takeaways from this chapter.

1. Change leaves an impact that is both positive and negative.

2. There is more information immediately available to more people than ever before.

3. We have been greatly influenced by the 3rd platform (industrial revolution).

4. Cloud computing, social media, data analytics, and greater mobility have redefined our personal and business worlds.

5. With change, our customers are expecting better, faster, and more impactful interactions and services.

6. We are learning that real-time data is a vital element in driving productivity.

7. Machine learning helps buyers make timely and accurate purchasing decisions.

8. Sensors are enabling statistical models of purchasing.

9. Today's markets are being influenced by factors like globalization and consolidation.

10. Buyers are looking for sellers to provide greater insight and awareness of resources and solutions.

11. Buyer-centered selling requires alignment of the buying and selling processes to ensure stakeholders get information, data, and documentation they need to make an informed decision.

12. Buyer-centered sellers bring a problem-solving approach to their sales calls and discussions.

13. Buyer-centered sellers show buyers that the current state is not a safe place to be. They provide concrete evidence of the gap between the current state and the future stare.

14. Sellers need to adapt their skills and competencies to the problem, opportunity, or threat facing the stakeholder.

15. Consensus builders unify stakeholders who hold disparate opinions or have reached conflicting conclusions.

## THE SKILL CHALLENGE

In order to become more effective and buyer-centered, what skill can you identify from the content in this chapter that requires practice on your part? Please write it here or on a separate sheet of paper.

## ADDENDUM 1: COMPARISON BETWEEN THE B2B BUYER AND THE B2B SELLER

| The New B2B Buyer | The New B2B Seller |
|---|---|
| Increased buyer knowledge | Provides relevant insight that provokes thought and educates |
| Greater number of buyers | Unifies support for change by differentiating the current state and the future state |
| Lengthy research phase | Engages stakeholders early and helps the buyer define and simplify the buying process |
| Greater reliance on self-diagnosis | Promotes alignment between the buying and selling processes to clarify choice and enrich decision-making |
| Expanding subscription economy | Recognizes that alternative financial models may offer tailored solutions to meet the buyers' needs |
| Formation of buying committees | Builds consensus around their solution and conveys the risk and cost of inaction |
| Trusted sources of information | Places more emphasis on net promoter scores and customer retention |
| Generational shift | Tech savvy pros who combine social media and relevant content with traditional modes (phone and E-mail) to their advantage |

# Chapter 2

# Get Connected: Adapt to the Customer's Buying Process

*"The way in which customers progress from the starting point to a purchase is unpredictable, inconsistent, and sometimes repetitive."*

Brent Adamson—Author of *The Challenger Customer*

## WHY SELLERS NEED TO UNDERSTAND THE CUSTOMER'S BUYING PROCESS

As consumers, every time we set out to make a major purchase (such as a car, house, vacation, or appliance) we begin a journey that will help us make the best decision for our money. We might prepare a budget, compare advertised prices, research warrantees, or read online reviews from customers. In other words, we conduct our own research to help us choose what we believe will be the best choice from the many options that are available. What happens when a sales representative tries to rush our decision or push us toward an option that doesn't fully meet our needs? We become confused, irritated, argumentative, or withdrawn; we stop listening and start looking at other alternatives.

For many of the same reasons that prompt us to undertake research and explore alternatives, organizations create buying processes in response to projects, "things they need to get done to achieve business goals. Buying is sometimes a component of these projects."[1] The buying process may include gathering information, interviewing potential suppliers, observing product demonstrations, conducting product trials, RFPs, laboratory tests, price comparisons, internal surveys, supplier certification, negotiations, and legal reviews. As sellers, if we ignore the buying process or attempt to rush the buying decision, we may find that potential customers push back, challenge our claims, or withdraw and become unresponsive. Buyers sense when we fail to respect their project prioritization, authority, responsibility, decision-making process, and culture. Even if our product or solution is clearly superior, we may find ourselves losing the opportunity because we have failed to respect internal processes, procedures, and protocols.

While a buying process may seem overly complex, demanding, and lengthy from the seller's perspective, companies create buying processes to cover a broad range of purchase decisions. If you (or your company) haven't mapped the process your customers go through to make a buying decision, you are just guessing, and guessing can cost you time, money, and market share.

Many sales organizations haven't taken the time to map and align the stages of the buying and selling process. Instead, sellers are sticking with the archaic notion that the only important stages are those in the selling process. Nothing could be further from the truth. Consider this situation.

### Story: Retail Security Systems

Amelia sells security systems to retailers in the Midwest. Her products and services help protect retail stores from theft and fire. On Tuesday, she received a phone call from a Regional Vice President of Markets for an automotive parts retailer in Minnesota. He wanted Amelia to give him a "ball park" quote on installing new security systems for six stores in the Minneapolis area. The two spent about 30 minutes covering some of the elements of the automotive aftermarket business. At the end of the conversation, the Vice President stated that he needed the quote and any supporting documentation by Friday for a meeting the following Monday with his CEO. Of course, the sales representative was eager to meet the requested deadline and saw the opportunity for a large sale that would help her exceed her quota. When she didn't receive a call back the next week and the VP didn't respond to her emails, she decided to make a list of what she didn't know that may have killed her opportunity. Here's her list.

— Why did he need the quote so quickly?

— What is their buying process, and how far along are the stakeholders in the journey?

— Who is their current supplier?

— Who was championing the current supplier?

— Are they considering other options as well?

— Why contact me at the last minute?

— Did they just want a quote to use in leveraging their current provider or another competitor?

— What insight or observation might I have offered that would have caused him to rethink such a quick decision?

Finish reading this chapter and see if you can determine where the stakeholder was in the buying process.

---

### The Challenge of Buyer-Centered Selling

***The Buyer's Dilemma:* Buyers face obstacles and barriers created by internal politics, competing initiatives, and different stakeholder agendas.** Each meeting can illustrate differences in urgency, priority, and preference. How can buyers bring insight and unity to the group while serving the business interests of all?

***The Seller's Challenge:* Sellers can become buyer-centered by adapting selling activities to the needs of the stakeholders, thereby simplifying the buying process.** Top sellers discover ways to help the buyer simplify the buying process. What information, research, or test results do stakeholders need to move confidently toward a buying commitment?

---

In this chapter, we explore the buying process and how that definition changes our dual focus of mapping the buying process and aligning selling activities to support the buying effort. We will also use the term "buyer(s)" and "stakeholder(s)" interchangeably.

## WHAT IS THE BUYING PROCESS: JOURNEY OR JOB?

While there are significant differences among and within organizations, we offer the following definition of a buying process: The actions and decisions that a buyer or group of buyers use to render a purchasing decision.

It may involve formal stages or steps that are sequenced to move the decision forward. Or, the process may be informal with a "We'll know it when we see it" attitude toward decision-making. In some organizations, the corporate culture requires certain formalities, while other organizations rely on experienced leaders to develop appropriate agendas to guide the group.

> A buying process is the actions and decisions that a buyer or group of buyers use to render a purchasing decision.

### What Are the Jobs to Be Done (JTBD)?

Often the steps in a company's buying process aren't really steps at all—they are functions that may be performed, dismissed, or repeated as needed until the "jobs" leading to a decision are completed. It's important to recognize that the composition of stakeholders or the expertise of buyers with the problem, opportunity, or threat (POT) can shorten or lengthen, simplify or complicate a buying process.

> JTBD are functions that may be performed, dismissed, or repeated as needed until the "jobs" leading to a decision are completed.

Over the last several years, writers have suggested a variety of tag words to describe the unique functions and activities of the "buying process." Is the process composed of steps or stages? Is the buying process simple and short or long and complicated? Some have described the buying process as a "journey." But what may appear to be a journey in one industry is a "quick trip to the corner" in another. Buying processes are like tomatoes. They come in different sizes, colors, shapes, and flavors.

One way to look at the buying process is as a series of "jobs to be done" (JTBD) on the behalf of the buying organization. In his book *The Innovator's Solution,* Clayton Christensen explains that sellers shouldn't view their objective as selling a product to a buyer but to help customers accomplish their JTBD.[2] Buyers don't just buy—that is only one aspect of their job. In most organizations, stakeholders work together to complete the purchase, implement the solution, and confirm that the promised benefits accrue to the buying organization. Each process can be considered one of the JTBD.

## How JTBD Changes the Seller's Perspective on Buying

When sellers view a sales opportunity from the buyer's perspective, they may see buying as a cluster of "jobs" that stakeholders have to complete in order to purchase, implement, and validate the final purchase. These jobs may require a strong bond between sales and customer service on the seller's side. It's vital that sellers assess the adequacy and alignment of resources. Inadequate resources can slowly drain the buyer's energy and commitment to the JTBD. Sellers can help buyers anticipate barriers, offer needed resources, and address alignment issues before they threaten the overall process.

Some buyers "don't know what to look at, how to organize themselves, or how to put in place a project plan to manage the difficulty in dealing with the unknown."[3] Examples include capital equipment, new software systems, embedded components, significant subscription services, and significant outsourcing of purchases.

Consider five ways a seller's understanding of JTBD helps the seller become buyer-centered. Each function expands and challenges how a seller and buyer can engage one another.

1. **Post-Sale Fulfillment.** The buyer's job many not end with the purchase of a product, service, or solution. The JTBD may include implementation and the application of performance metrics. The buyer may need the seller's support and leadership to ensure that implementation and initial deployment are successful. Procurement may welcome a seller taking responsibility for measuring post-sales adoption, compliance, and business results.

2. **Common Focus on Value.** The importance of the JTBD doesn't lie with the product to be purchased; it depends on the product's contribution to business outcomes. ("It's not the drill; it's the hole.") In other words, the JTBD tells the seller what value the buyer expects from the purchase. The JTBD process helps the buyer look beyond the purchase order or the letter of intent.

3. **Mutual Concern with Resources.** The buyer's JTBD can be challenged or disrupted by poor alignment of resources to support the job. The seller would benefit greatly from tracking the availability of buyer resources to support completion of the job. Is the buyer getting "what" they need "when" they need it?

4. **Joint Approach to Obstacles.** Unanticipated obstacles may surface and stall or derail the JTBD. Suppose the launch of a new product by the buying organization doesn't go as expected. Does the product failure compromise the budget for this project? What happens if the organization decides to decrease or freeze spending? Will it affect this sale?

5. **Common Focus on Job-Related Measures.** The buyer and buying organization may be focused on job-related measures instead of product performance measures. This could be a "game changer" for the seller who is used to quoting product features and reporting arcane test results. For example, a seller may claim the "speed" of their product will increase the speed with which the buyer serves his customer. But what if the buyer is trying to "treat the customer better" not "faster"? "Speed" is a feature of the product while "making

the customer feel welcome and taking the time to answer questions" is what the organization is trying to achieve. In this case, a product feature may not match with the real JTBD.

## CORE ELEMENTS OF THE BUYING PROCESS

Our objective here is to define and apply core elements that will aid the understanding and mapping of the buying process.

1. **Core Issues.** Core Issues are the three questions cited and described in Figure 2-1. These are the basic questions underlying a buyer's research, conversations, and group deliberation.

   a. **"Why Change?"** is about gaining agreement among stakeholders that there is a compelling reason to do something different, such as change suppliers or engage external resources. It's all about change or "no change."

   b. **"Why Change Now?"** is about urgency and priority. Is the problem, opportunity, or threat (POT) important enough to require immediate action from the buying organization? The willingness to act must outweigh the perceived cost of inaction.

   c. **"Who Will Do It Best?"** is all about differentiating options or solutions, showing proof that the vendor can deliver results, and mitigating risk that may cloud the thinking of buyers and stakeholders.

2. **Jobs to Be Done (JTBD).** These "jobs" are what some writers refer to as "stages." In this model, we identify six jobs. Buyers may have more or fewer jobs, depending on the complexity of the buying process. Some jobs may be addressed concurrently, while others require repeated efforts to satisfy the requirements of the job. Buyers can also work on several JTBD simultaneously. Every action the buyer or stakeholder takes should tie back to one of the six jobs.

3. **Tasks.** Buying and selling tasks are not shown on Figure 2-1 but are vital to overall mapping. Tasks are activities that sellers or buyers

undertake in order to complete a job. This may include research, interviews, product tests, calculations of KPIs, and the like.

4.  **Exit Criteria**. In mapping a buyer's process, exit criteria are clear indicators that a customer has advanced from one purchase stage to the next.[4] They are requirements that must be met to move to the next stage. We will discuss this more later in the chapter. The better the seller's understanding of the core elements from the buyer's perspective, the more accurate the seller's map is likely to be.

Figure 2-1 is a generic overview of the buying process and serves to illustrate the core elements. Ultimately, it provides the seller a guideline for mapping the buying process of a target organization.

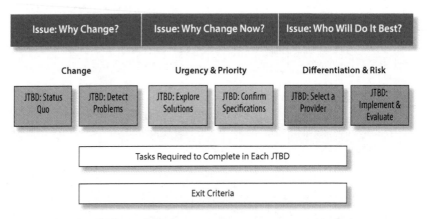

Figure 2-1: Overview of a Buying Process

Let's delve a little deeper into jobs and tasks, because they are critical to mapping.

Every buying process includes two key elements that determine the direction, speed, and outcome of the decision process: "Jobs" and "Tasks." A job is something that buyers need to accomplish, or it is something they see as essential to moving the buying process forward. Each job may involve one or more tasks for completion. Let's consider an example. A job might be to "Select a Provider." The task might be to "research and report on how other internal groups have scored and evaluated suppliers," to "determine which supplier is best able to satisfy our requirements," or, it might be to "evaluate how other products compare to our current solution."

Some tasks may be "assigned out" or delegated to a sub-group. Other tasks may be accomplished with a few minutes of discussion or a quick telephone call. Sellers should understand that some stakeholders are included in the buying process in order to facilitate completion of a specific task.

It may sound simple, but the outlining of a buying process can be treacherous and complicated. If buyers focus on tasks that do not help accomplish the JTBD, they will waste time, and the process may slow or stall. Too extensive an outline of tasks can have a similar impact on job completion. Experienced buyers will be talented project and process managers who delegate and meet deadlines, anticipate barriers, and plan for needed resources.

## Components of Change

1. **JTBD: Status Quo.** The Status Quo (or "current state") is not a phase in the selling process; it is a stage or starting point in the buying process. It is a condition that may predicate action, depending on which of three conditions the stakeholder finds him or herself in. These three conditions are comfort, curiosity, and concern. In the comfort condition, stakeholders are passive, believing all is well and no extraordinary action is required. They believe no change is required. In curiosity, stakeholders are interested in knowing more about their current condition. They are attentive but unwilling to consider change at this juncture. When stakeholders are concerned, they sense that the level of risk has increased. Accordingly, they are vigilant and poised to take action if threats or opportunities materialize.

   Let's take an example. A department head led a product review process three years ago. As she took a retrospective look back in time, she was very impressed by the supplier's customer service. It was a deciding factor in awarding the business. But the situation has changed. There have been subtle changes in service. Shipments delayed. The supplier has changed the customer service representative. Small disappointments have built up, and the buyer has transitioned from comfort to curiosity and then to concern.

Each stakeholder's view of the Status Quo is influenced by feedback (customer reviews, performance measures, technical reports) on how well the existing product is functioning. Often, feedback on existing products begins with employees who use the products frequently. These "users" can be instrumental in launching a buying process or staying the course with existing products.

**Example Tasks.** The task for the seller is to raise concerns with the Status Quo by helping the buyer recognize there are problems or threats that can adversely affect business outcomes or opportunities that should be pursued. Sellers can provide insight that opens the buyer's perspective and resonates with one or more buyers. The seller that provides the insight can become the anchor for the solution. The task for the buyer is to be willing to have a conversation or to read some information that might change their thinking.

2. **JTBD: Detect Problems.** A buyer might attempt to "detect problems" by asking, "Is there a problem, opportunity, or threat emerging that would warrant change in how we source this product or service?" Often, a buying process commences when a stakeholder reads an article, blog, or eBook, listens to a webinar, or attends a trade show. Some authors have referred to this as a "trigger event." This is an event that causes the buyer to envision a clear need for change along with a sense of urgency.

> A Trigger Event is an event that causes the buyer to envision a clear need for change along with a sense of urgency.

For example, you sense your hard drive may be failing, and you realize your data is not backed up to an external drive. You do not want to chance losing your data, so you immediately look for a solution.

In this case, your fear of an impending "trigger event" prompts you to seek a solution quickly.

**Example Tasks.** The buyer may feel it's necessary to interview other company "users" and ask for their input. Another task might be to ask for a technical assessment from IT. Could they provide backup and how long would it take to transfer data?

Whatever the source, it is sufficiently provocative if it causes the individual or group to take a closer look at the unmet needs of their organization. There is a growing realization that they must do something. The prospect is asking, "Is this an 'irritating, important, or critical problem?'"[5]

The buyer may assign some tasks to an external resource (like a consultant) to determine whether problems are real, recurrent, or temporary. Some buyers task internal specialists to determine the size, scope, and urgency of the problem or threat. Others conduct studies to estimate the revenue potential of any growth option.

## The Roots of Urgency & Priority

3. **JTBD: Explore Solutions.** Once a problem, opportunity, or threat has been identified, the buyer begins to look for solutions that are available in the marketplace. They review the web for published literature and third-party reviews, peruse supplier websites, conduct internal and external peer discussions, and often engage with suppliers' sales personnel.

   At this point, the stakeholders expand their studies to all interested parties. They often include Procurement and members of the technical team to identify potential suppliers, review their credentials, and explore the fit between the needs of the buying organization and product capabilities. Because of the diversity of stakeholder interests, conflicting information may exist. During this stage, it is not uncommon for one or more stakeholders to have a preferred vendor in mind.

**Example Tasks.** One common task is to rely on members of the buying team or users to identify characteristics of a quality solution. They could search for available information on options. Research by Forrester showed that nearly three-fourths of buying decisions ultimately were awarded to the supplier that first helped shape the prospect's vision of a solution.[6]

4. **JTBD: Confirm Specifications.** In this stage, stakeholders begin formulating an image of what is necessary by defining "What exactly do we want the solution to do for us? How quickly must it address our needs? What would it cost? What quantitative outcomes can we expect?" This will enable the seller to build fundamental financial models for the stakeholder. Stakeholders also ask, "What specifications and expectations should we formalize for our solution? How do we assemble the expertise (internal and external) to answer our questions?" They may decide to develop and send out Request for Proposals (RFPs) or inquiries to engage suppliers. They may receive proposals from qualified suppliers and review them. Stakeholders may also request online or in-person product demonstrations. These will enable the seller to discover the stakeholder's requirements.

   **Example Tasks.** An appropriate task for the buying team might be to identify the criteria for an ideal solution or send an RFP to potential suppliers.

## Differentiation & Risk Factors

5. **JTBD: Select a Provider.** This stage can become automatic when a supplier has capabilities that align with the newly recognized needs. The key question that stakeholders will ask is, "Does this solution do what we want it to do?" The selection process can become long and complicated, however, when live supplier presentations or product trials are required. In every organization, there is an internal selection process. Some are subjective, and some are objective and may include supplier scorecards to compare solutions.

**Example Tasks.** At this phase, risk mitigation is paramount. Stakeholders will seek to avoid risk through social validation with peers who have worked with the supplier, by reviewing industry influencer recommendations and testimonials, by requiring guarantees, or by conducting product trials. Suppliers will also focus on how thorough the implementation plan is—post purchase.

With most complex B2B deals, there is also a period of negotiation when both parties need to agree on price, terms, and conditions. Ultimately the buying organization issues a purchase order, a contract, a consulting services agreement, or an irrevocable letter of credit, or they decide to stay with the incumbent.

6. **JTBD: Implement & Evaluate.** During this phase, the stakeholder is laser focused on ensuring that their day-to-day operations are not disrupted by unexpected difficulties resulting from implementation.

   **Example Tasks.** Buyers will monitor key performance indicators (KPIs) to ensure that the seller is performing according to the agreed upon timelines and schedules. Often they will schedule supplier reviews to ensure financial metrics are being achieved.

## KEYS TO MAPPING YOUR CUSTOMER'S BUYING PROCESS

There are 10 keys that will help sellers uncover a company's buying process and lay the foundation for buyer-centered selling.

1. **Capture the JTBD in the Buyer's Terminology.** What is the overall business outcome that the buyer wants to accomplish? By focusing on the JTBD, the seller will be better positioned to understand the initiatives that are of value to the buyer and the organization.

2. **Uncover the Buyer's Problem, Opportunity, or Threat.** Stakeholders don't buy products; they buy solutions to business problems. Sellers should search for gaps in expected performance levels and determine what the buyer hopes to achieve and how will they measure progress

toward achievement. Sellers must show buyers the clear difference between their current state and an improved future state.

3. **Expect Shifts Forward and Back.** The JTBD are not necessarily linear. Buyers and stakeholders may move forward and then back as they attempt to get clarity on how to address or resolve their issue. Many factors may contribute to regression. "A new and influential stakeholder may join the buying process and re-examine a previous decision. A persuasive sales person may convince the stakeholder group that they need to revisit their decision criteria, or the emergence of another competing project could be seen as more urgent."[7] Internal and external conditions may impact the buying organization's priorities. They may learn new information from your competitor or their due diligence. When stakeholders' resolve to move forward regresses, the seller needs to identify what actions are required to re-energize the process.

4. **Different Buyers May Be at Different Issues/Stages.** During the buying processes, stakeholders may be at different stages. Why? Some buyers move faster through the process, some are slower and more meticulous, and others may desire to stay in one stage until they can answer all relevant questions. When a committee is involved, stakeholders process information and reach conclusions in different timeframes. In some organizations, decisions are reached without a formalized process. This can lead stakeholders on an unpredictable journey and make it difficult for sellers to track and cover all stakeholders.

5. **Unseen Forces May Be at Work.** Political factors, competing projects, and changes in group membership can slow or confuse the buying process.

6. **Lack of Experience Can Plague a Committee.** Perhaps your product is one that is purchased every five to seven years. Technology can change products, capabilities, warrantees, and prices quickly. Stakeholders may find it difficult to move forward on an issue. Buyer-centered sellers are quick to offer prescriptive guidance to map and guide stakeholders through the process.

7. **Consensus Can Be a Challenge.** It may be difficult to discover the sources of disagreements. It may take a skilled seller to bring people together to build a consensus. Sellers would be wise to ask the stakeholders if they have a buying process. If they don't have a buying process, sellers would be wise to suggest one. Explain typical jobs, tasks, or issues that other organizations have used to reach a decision on your product or solution. Rather than becoming "just-in-time information concierges" who support the customers in their chaotic buying process, the real job of the salesperson is to help remove the complexity and chaos and enable the customer to manage their journey more effectively.[8] Be a resource and a trusted advisor.

8. **Look for Exit Criteria.** Moving through the JTBD, requires "buyer actions" that complete each stage and ready the stakeholders for the next task in the JTBD. Typically, we have called these buyer actions "exit criteria." These also mark a change in the probability of a seller winning the sale. The exit criteria should include the following characteristics: First, the buyer should take actions that show commitment to moving the buying process forward. Second, these actions should be specific and measurable, and they should move the buyer away from "status quo." Here is an example: "The issue, possible cause, and business requirements have been defined and documented to us in writing."

9. **Transitions Can Cause Confusion.** Most buyers are not clear about how to move from the acknowledgment of the problem to the solution. To smooth this transition, sellers should bring specific information, tailored to each stakeholder according to the stage they are in or to the task they are addressing. On average, 6.8 people are involved in today's B2B purchase decisions.[9] It can be difficult to meet the disparate needs of stakeholders at different points in the process. One of the ways to remove complexity is to create a joint activity plan that identifies who is responsible for conducting each activity by the agreed upon timeline.

10. **Each Core Issue Involves Three Types of Vital Tasks.** During the buying process, stakeholders continually perform discovery, collaboration, and validation to promote consensus.

### What's the Downside of not Aligning Buying and Selling?

It's easy for sellers to surge ahead of the customer. What happens when the buy/sell processes aren't aligned?

- Sellers aren't positioned to provide insight to the stakeholders because they don't understand the issues the buyer wants addressed.
- Sellers become frustrated because stakeholders appear to be "dragging their feet."
- Stakeholders view sellers as pushy or unresponsive.
- The buy-sell cycle gets longer and longer because sellers aren't positioned to help the stakeholders overcome buying obstacles.
- Stakeholders get frustrated and decide the status quo is their best decision.
- Stakeholders go silent when they believe you don't understand their problem, opportunity, or threat, or when they don't believe you are adding value.
- Deals that are forecast to close often go to "no decision" and ultimately to a loss.

"When uncertainty exists, delays happen. When delays happen, priorities shift. When priorities shift, opportunities can disappear."[10]

## WHAT CHALLENGES DO SELLERS FACE IN ALIGNING PROCESSES?

Each Core Issue raises potential challenges for the seller. Consider a brief overview of challenges that may surface in a complex sale.

### Core Issue: "Why Change?"

**Status Quo:** While entrenched in the status quo, the prospect may have the perspective that "things are good." They aren't looking for change. Status quo looks great. In fact, they may be ignoring obvious signals that circumstances are deteriorating. The challenge facing the seller is to promote awareness by providing insight that changes their perspective and makes them see a problem, opportunity, or threat. Engage the stakeholder(s). Become a conduit for new information.

Mike Kunkle, a well-respected author, describes the value of a seller's insight in this way: "… information or an idea that is based on credible research, authoritative content, or relevant experiences, which, when personalized to your client's likely or known challenges and opportunities and shared appropriately, opens your client's mind to think about their situation in a new way and shows them a path toward solving a challenge or capitalizing on an opportunity through your company's capabilities and differentiators."[11]

### Buyer-Centered Sellers Can Help:

1. To create a dialogue (through a phone call, email, social outreach, or other means) that helps the prospect overcome the feeling that "all is well."

2. To share information and additional insight that would elevate the prospect's interest beyond curiosity and move them to realize they have a problem. Current data on trends, benchmarks, as well as original published research from credible sources can change buyers' perspectives quickly.

**Detect Problems:** As stakeholders begin to detect problems, they may begin to see the risks or flaws in the strategy of continuing with the current solution. There is enough information to warrant a review. "A problem, opportunity, or threat may well exist, and we need to get a handle on it quickly."

### Buyer-Centered Sellers Can Help:

1. Provide insight that elevates stakeholder concern. Often these may be done through social media, white papers, analyst reports, webinars, eBooks, or blogs, to cite a few examples. Many stakeholders may recognize that a problem, opportunity, or threat exists but want confirmation that others within the organization have the same level of concern. They want to do something, but they are unsure what steps to take. Sellers may promote a discovery process that uncovers the problem or a validation process that documents the problem's existence.

2. To promote validation and consensus while providing a road map to lead the buyer or buying group from "Why Change?" to "Why Change Now?"

### Core Issue: "Why Change Now?"

**Explore Solutions:** As stakeholders explore solutions, it's logically plausible that someone outside the organization may have a better perspective on the problem, opportunity, or threat. This affords the seller an excellent opportunity to provide insight and experience that lead to change.

By defining the size and scope and the time horizon of a problem, opportunity, or threat, a stakeholder can grasp the total impact on their business processes and customer relationships. They can better grasp the economic consequences of doing nothing.

### Buyer-Centered Sellers Can Help:

1. Navigate the minefield of options by showing shortcomings, barriers, and implications.

2. Provide insight into the size, scope, and urgency of a problem or a looming threat.

3. Calculate the "cost of doing nothing." From the seller perspective, the selling goal of the JTBD is to solicit a commitment from the buyer to abandon the current solution.

**Confirm Specifications:** In the Confirm Specifications discussion, prospective buyers may be receptive to internal specialists with product knowledge that identifies the specifications necessary for an effective solution. Buyers may engage third-party sources (such as channel partners and consultants, peers, and colleagues, both within and external to the organization) to validate their portrait of a successful solution. Stakeholders will turn to users and specialists to refine the list of essential elements in a solution. Prospective buyers often want product demonstrations and usage trials. The buying team may develop comparison profiles on available solutions along with a risk profile of making a change. At the end of the "Why Change Now?" discussion, many buying teams generate a scorecard or checklist for judging the quality of a solution.

Sellers help stakeholders through the buying process by crafting realistic expectations for the ideal solution and by applying measures of value and performance. This is also an opportunity to plant seeds for decision criteria that may be used to differentiate solutions in the next stage.

At this point in the buying process, many stakeholders feel they have a firm grip on what they need.

## Core Issue: "Who Will Do It Best?"

**Select a Provider:** In the Select a Provider discussion, stakeholders begin to evaluate suppliers and scorecard solutions. Often "scorecarding" occurs after a usage trial, an RFP, or a committee presentation. Many qualification processes are formal and complex, with a rigid set of criteria and a weighting system to insure objectivity. Other processes are more akin to a "beauty pageant," during which suppliers are expected to court the stakeholders in a committee setting, followed by a vote.

Sellers tend to view this stage as a quick vote or telephone call, but that's not always the case. Stakeholders often have questions, challenge claims, or request additional documentation. They may want to review an implementation plan or explore customer service issues. The seller should be prepared to respond to questions, planning issues, concerns, pricing, and requests for references. Sellers should help buyers discover timely information about their solution that differentiates them from those offered by competitors. It's vital that sellers continue to help the stakeholders see measurable and personal value in the proposed solution.

### Buyer-Centered Sellers Can Help:

1.  Provide logic using facts, data, reasoning, proof, and evidence to help buyers justify their decision.

2.  Mitigate risk and post purchase anxiety i.e., "did we make the right decision" by providing ample proof sources such as financial measures of Return on Investment (ROI), Internal Rate of Return (IRR), Net Present Value (NPV) or Payback, customer testimonials, or customer or supplier site visits. Proof sources will help the buyer gain consensus with a thorough implementation plan.

3.  Negotiate the price, terms and conditions. Sellers should assure stakeholders that the selling organization is prepared to handle any legal or financial issues with flexibility. This may involve a formal or informal negotiating process surrounding price or financial terms. It's never over until the purchase order (PO) has been released or the contract is signed.

At this stage, some sales opportunities are awarded with "paperwork to follow." But that isn't always the case. More than a few deals have been lost because of unexpected legal or financial inflexibilities.

**Implement & Evaluate:** During the Implement and Evaluate discussion, the seller ensures a smooth implementation of their product or service along with a post-sale support plan. This requires a carefully monitored transition plan, extensive product and service training, or new workflow development and procedures. A detailed implementation plan is required to eliminate inadvertent errors, delays, productivity issues, increased costs, poor employee morale, and a breakdown in the seller's hard-earned relationship with the buying organization. The Implement and Evaluate stage is often the most overlooked and undervalued in the buying process. Often the seller prematurely moves on to the next sale or provides a handoff to someone else in the organization that is less than ideal.

Sellers may experience a rude awakening when products are returned, future scheduled orders are canceled, and payment is delayed or refused. The primary objective of the seller is to assure a smooth transition that leads to customer retention, referrals, and repeat business.

## Buyer-Centered Sellers Can Help:

1. Arrange a kickoff meeting with the seller's implementation team. Cover the buyer's objectives along with key metrics that are important to each stakeholder and why they chose your solution. Then set up a telephone call with the client to introduce the implementation team and officially handoff the implementation process to them.

2. Develop an implementation plan that is agreed upon by both parties. Include timelines, responsibilities, and contact information for everyone involved.

3. Coordinate an introduction of the seller's implementation team to stakeholders.

4. Monitor "tasks" by both teams to ensure that each commitment is fulfilled.

Every buyer or buying group has a predictable pathway they follow to make a purchasing decision. It is incumbent upon sellers to map the buying process or suggest an approach to the buyers and then align their selling activity in a manner that will elevate the seller's position and speed the process.

### Story: Retail Security Systems Part 2

Now let's return to our story of Amelia, the security systems seller. If you remember, she responded to a price quotation request. Clearly, the buyer was in the Selection stage, evaluating options by price. Amelia

attempted to be helpful by quoting him a price without understanding the stages in the buying process and the alignment of buying and
selling. What stages did the Regional Vice President go through to get
to this point? She didn't have enough information to know if he was
"price shopping." However, we do know that she pitched the product
and a price to win the deal without having a firm understanding of
what the RVP wanted to accomplish. Amelia had little understanding of
the RVP's ideal solution. She developed good questions, but they were
developed after she had delivered a quote.

## BENEFITS OF MAPPING AND ALIGNING THE BUY-SELL PROCESSES

When you map the customer's buying process accurately and align sales
activities with the information, insight, documentation and perspective needed by stakeholders, you become a guide or navigator for the
customer's buying efforts. You become a seller who helps them solve a
problem, capitalize on an opportunity, or mitigate a risk rather than
pushing a solution.

Another benefit of mapping and aligning the buy-sell processes is
that sellers gain an understanding of where each stakeholder is in their
buying process. Based on the questions a stakeholder asks, a seller can
ascertain what stage or what "jobs to be done" area each stakeholder is in.
Remember, most stakeholders self-educate before they engage with you.
Once they engage, they are also talking to other stakeholders within and
external to their organization; they are also talking to your competitors,
and they are receiving and reviewing a stockpile of information—often
simultaneously.

In Figure 2-1, we gave you a generic overview of the buying process
and the core elements. Figure 2-2 shows our view of the Buy-Sell Process
for more complex and expensive B2B products. Both Figures 2-1 and 2-2
underscore the principle that sellers should provide a road map to help the
customer buy.

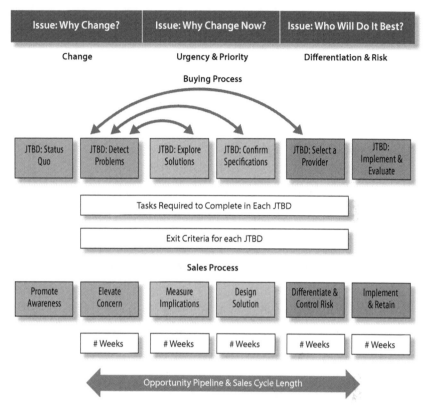

Figure 2-2: The Buy-Sell Process for Complex, Expensive B2B Products

*(The format and content of Figures 2-1 and 2-2 were influenced by several sources, including publications by Gartner and the work of Neil Rackham).*

Consider these benefits to buy-sell process mapping and alignment:

1. **Visibility of All Opportunities:** Once a complex opportunity has been recorded in the CRM system, it has visibility to other sales professionals, management, and sales operations. Sellers know exactly where the sales opportunity is in the sales process. Managers know where each sales opportunity is in the funnel, the currency amount, the length of time for each of the JTBD, conversion ratios, and the required next steps. Unfortunately, the CRM sales process stages don't always align with the buying process stages.

2. **Road map of Buying Activity:** By suggesting a buying process, sellers will aid stakeholders who may not have a process in place. They may be unfamiliar with your product or a similar one. This step also helps sellers build a road map for selling activity that supports how buyers buy. Managers can use the process to mentor and coach to best practices.

3. **Onboarding & Ramp-Up:** Having a defined buying process allows new sales representatives to ramp up quickly and be more productive in the near term.

4. **Improved Close Ratio:** If the buying process is defined properly, then coaching will be more effective, and win rates should improve.

5. **Identify Stalled Opportunities:** A formal buying process will show where sales opportunities get stuck or lost. This provides an opportunity for coaching to improve specific selling skills.

6. **Improved Predictive Accuracy:** It's always a best practice to walk the stakeholder(s) through their buying process and how you will support them. This allows the seller to ensure the opportunity is a good fit for their time, and it allows each stakeholder to make a series of micro commitments (a commitment at each stage or during each job to be done and defined by the exit criteria that moves the process forward) before they make a formal commitment to purchase at the end of the process.

7. **Promotes Consensus.** There are many components of group buying decisions that must be present for a group to reach a consensus on what solution to purchase. First, stakeholders must believe that the solution in question solves the problem at hand and that your team has the skills and commitment to solve the problem. Second, stakeholders must believe that the solution is affordable. Third, there must be a credible ROI. Fourth, stakeholders must believe that the problem, opportunity, or threat is urgent and requires timely action. Fifth, the supplier must offer a "proof point" that convinces the buyer of the validity of the seller's claims. Sixth, there must be an emotional connection where

the buyers believe in you, your product, and your company's ability to deliver the results desired. Last, the discussion process must allow and encourage the resolution of all concerns and reservations.

8. **Stakeholder Focus.** Different stakeholders can be at different points in understanding the problem, opportunity or threats, and options. When sellers ignore these differences, it can create barriers to closing the deal.

## Key Points to Remember for Buyer-Centered Sellers

1. Managers and sellers must understand their customers' buying processes. The buying process serves as a foundation for the selling activity.

2. The buying process answers three simple questions that we identify as Core Issues: "Why Change? (Change)" "Why Do It Now? (Urgency & Priority)" "Who Will Do It Best? (Differentiation & Risk Mitigation)."

3. Each selling team needs to map their customers' buying processes and suggest a buying process.

4. The typical buying process includes the following Jobs to Be Done: Status Quo, Detect Problems, Explore Solutions, Confirm Specifications, Select a Provider, and Implement and Evaluate.

5. There are more stakeholders involved in a major decision than ever before, requiring greater resources from the seller while challenging the project management skills of the buyer.

6. Sellers need to understand where each stakeholder is in the buying process. It is not uncommon for different stakeholders to be in different positions in the buying stages or Jobs to Be Done stage. Buyers can regress or be in multiple Jobs to Be Done categories simultaneously.

7. With complex and expensive B2B solutions, the stakeholders must collaborate and agree that a problem, opportunity, or threat exists and agree its importance is high enough to act.

8. With complex and expensive B2B solutions, the stakeholders often must reach consensus before they will agree to act.

9. Often the buying and selling processes become misaligned—one moves ahead of the other.

10. Every buying stage has an exit point that requires measurable action to be taken by a stakeholder that enables everyone to proceed to the next stage or to the next Job to Be Done.

11. Buying is not linear. No one ever said that one or more buyers cannot recede to a prior stage or that all buyers are in the same stage simultaneously. See Addendum 3.

12. Addendum 4 shows that buying is often chaotic because each stakeholder receives input and stimuli from a variety of internal and external sources consistently and simultaneously.

13. Sellers should analyze where their deals get stuck and take appropriate action.

14. The buying process should be revisited at least every year.

## THE SKILL CHALLENGE

In order to become more effective and buyer centered, what skill can you identify from the content in this chapter that requires skill and practice? Please write it here or on a separate sheet of paper.

## ADDENDUM 2: QUESTIONS SELLERS SHOULD ASK THEMSELVES ABOUT THE CUSTOMER'S BUYING PROCESS

1. What events have prompted stakeholders to question the adequacy of the status quo?

2. Is this challenge a problem, opportunity, or threat for the customer's organization?

3. What is the level of urgency and priority surrounding this issue?

4. Have you defined all the internal and external stakeholders?

5. Do all the stakeholders agree with the cost of inaction and the need to do something?

6. Have you shown clear differences between the current state, the future state, and the gap in between (cost of inaction)?

7. Do you understand the cause of the gap?

8. Has the buying organization made similar purchasing decisions before? What steps did they take to decide?

9. Is there a timeline for making a buying decision (a "buying window")?

10. Will the buying organization issue an RFP, RFQ, or RFI?

11. How and when will suppliers communicate with stakeholders?

12. What is their decision-making process?

13. Will they utilize a scorecard to evaluate each supplier?

14. What will be the outcome of the buying process? A decision? An advisory report or referral? A recommendation?

15. Are there related processes underway that may slow, speed, or alter this buying process?

16. Can you foster collaboration among the stakeholders at each stage of the buying process or the Jobs to Be Done?

17. Buyers and Sellers use different resources throughout the buy-sell process. See Addendums 5 and 6 for some examples.

## ADDENDUM 3: QUESTIONS A SALES MANAGER SHOULD ASK THEIR TEAM ABOUT THE CUSTOMER'S BUYING PROCESS

1. Has your selling team mapped the stakeholders' buying process or shared with them an appropriate buying process map?

2. Are your sellers using discovery throughout the buying process?

3. Are your sellers promoting collaboration amongst the stakeholders at each buying stage or Jobs to Be Done stage?

4. Will the seller be able to create consensus and unify stakeholders to support your company's solution?

5. Is the customer's buying process described in your company CRM?

6. Do your sellers use the buying process consistently in conducting selling activities?

7. For each sales opportunity, is there proper alignment of the buying and selling processes?

8. Does everyone in sales, marketing, and the organization speak the language of the customer's buying process?

9. Do you use the buying process during your coaching sessions (especially deal reviews) to improve each seller's win rate?

10. Do your sellers review and update the buying process on a yearly basis?

## ADDENDUM 4: ANOTHER VIEW OF THE BUYING PROCESS: NON-LINEAR

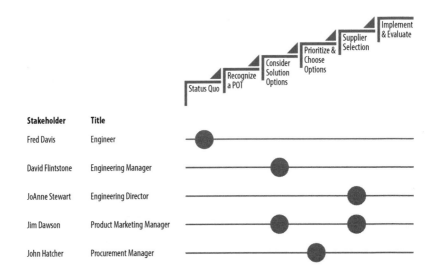

This diagram illustrates two important points. First, the buying process is not linear. Second, different stakeholders can be in different JTBD areas and in more than one area simultaneously.

## ADDENDUM 5: ANOTHER VIEW OF THE BUYING PROCESS: CHAOTIC

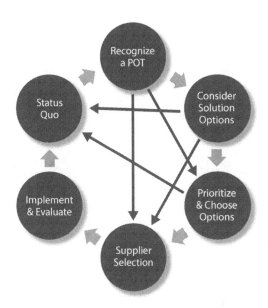

This diagram illustrates several important facts:

1. A buyer can Recognize that a Problem, Opportunity, or Threat (POT) exists and then go to Prioritize & Choose Options or another JTBD while skipping Consider Solution Options.

2. A buyer can skip stages or JTBD, i.e., go from Recognize a POT to a Supplier Selection based on research or familiarity.

3. A buyer can choose to go back to Status Quo at any time.

4. A buyer can go back and forth from one JTBD to another, e.g., from Consider Solution Options to Supplier Selection, etc.

## ADDENDUM 6: RESOURCES OFTEN USED DURING THE BUYING PROCESS

| General Categories | Education & Thought Leadership | | Solutions | Experience & Expertise | Proof |
|---|---|---|---|---|---|
| Jobs to Be Done | Detect Problems | Explore Options | Confirm Specifications | Select a Provider | Implement & Use |
| Content and Activities to Share | General Web Search | Peruse Supplier Websites | Supplier Demo | Site Visit | Implementation Plan |
| | White Papers & Case Studies | Third Party Reviews | Product Trials | Customer Testimonials | Kickoff Meeting |
| | Webinars. Podcasts & Videos | RFP Creation | Supplier Scorecard | Customer References | User Surveys |
| | Buying Team Formation | RFP Response Comparisons | External Stakeholder Discussion | Financial Analysis | Scheduled Supplier Meetings |
| | Data Analysis | Discussion with Users | Risk Profile | Buying Team Decision | Data Analysis |
| | Feasibility Studies | Comparison Studies | Buying Team Review | External Pricing Benchmarks | |
| | Discussion with Users | Buying Team Discussion | | | |
| | Analyst Research Reports | Buyer Guides | | | |
| | Social Media | Data Sheets | | | |
| | Industry Articles | | | | |
| | Industry Position Statements | | | | |

Note: These are examples of common resources used by buyers during the buying process by the JTBD. The resources used may change by industry, buyer, and JTBD.

## ADDENDUM 7: RESOURCES OFTEN USED DURING THE SELLING PROCESS

| General Categories | Education & Thought Leadership | | Solutions | Experience & Expertise | Proof |
|---|---|---|---|---|---|
| Jobs to Be Done | Detect Problems | Explore Solutions | Confirm Specifications | Select a Provider | Implement & Use |
| Content to Share | Social Media | Cost of Inaction | Presentation Deck | Term Sheet | Implementation Plan |
| | White Papers & Case Studies | RFP Template | Product Demo | Standard Contract | Company Profile Form |
| | Blogs | Comparison Studies | Product Trial Evaluation Form | Pricing | Standard Survey |
| | eBooks | Third Party Analyst Reports | Committee Presentation Outline | Third Party Analyst Reports | Business Review Form |
| | Webinars & Podcasts | How to Information | Case Studies | ROI Calculator | |
| | Feature Articles | | | Product Trial Evaluation Form | |
| | Technology News | | | eSignatures | |
| | Diagnostic Tools | | | | |

Note: These are examples of common resources used by sellers to help buyers facilitate their buying process by the JTBD. The resources used may change by industry, buyer, and JTBD.

# Chapter 3

# The Tortoise and the Hare: Win with Buyer-Centered Discovery

"Asking questions to understand what buyers value is a smart strategy for sellers. By asking just one or two questions to understand what an individual values and the hierarchy or priority of what is valued, a seller demonstrates that he or she cares about the unique buyer."

Deb Calvert—Author of *DISCOVER Questions® Get You Connected*

A t times, sellers are the victims of conflicting messages. On one hand, they are pressured by sales leadership to shorten the sales cycle and preserve their most precious resource—time. But there are other contrary messages that remind sellers to "cover your bases," "don't leave any stone unturned," and cultivate strong, long-term relationships. Should we be quick or slow? As sellers, are we more like the tortoise or the hare?

For many sellers, the answer is simple: it's easier to be fast and shortcut the selling efforts than to overindulge in an opportunity and deny other prospects the attention necessary to win. For some sellers, that is absolutely the correct choice. Why? The sales opportunity is either heavily weighted for or against the seller, and the investment of additional time seems unnecessary. Or, the buying process involves one or two stakeholders, and decisions normally take only a few days or a week at the outside.

However, there are other sales opportunities that include a large group of buyers or influencers and a deliberation process filled with demonstrations, product assessments, and the careful review of business cases. Some sellers dread "the long road," while others thrive in guiding a buying process that takes months, a year, or even longer.

When the sales opportunity requires a long sales cycle, shortcuts, "silver bullets," and a quick pitch will leave the Hare on the outside wondering what went wrong. This is a clear home court advantage for the Tortoise.

Top performers rely on sales skills and a tool often overlooked by others: the discovery process. Mike Kunkle, a prolific author and evangelist for sales transformation, explains that improving sales discovery skills is the best method of improving the average seller's performance.[1]

Several years ago, a friend shared a story about a seller and her diligent approach to sales discovery as she attempted to sell a significant and complex piece of business.

### Story: The "Right Place at the Right Time" Sale

The seller, an IT specialist from the Midwest, made a sales call to a large but unlikely "suspect." The outcome of the sales call created a story that is legendary. On that day in late February outside of Detroit, the seller found herself in "the right place at the right time." Her suspect (later prospect) explained that the company had purchased several smaller companies over the last few years and was planning a complete overhaul of their data centers to capitalize on cost reductions. The company's plan was to combine six data centers into one or two, depending on the financial and performance implications.

Now the bad news: the parent company had a long-standing relationship with an IT vendor out of the Northeast. When asked to describe the vendor, the buyer explained that they were rock solid, dependable, conservative, and cautious. "Quite frankly, for us to drive revenue, improve market share, and contain costs, we need to be a bit more aggressive."

With the buyer's permission, she undertook an exhaustive sales discovery process. She interviewed all stakeholders in the Detroit center, explored their vision, and probed for preferences, priorities, and measurable outcomes. But she didn't limit her discovery to the home office. She sought permission (that was granted) to visit other offices, data centers, and executives. At the end of every week, she wrote a report of her findings and sent her thoughts to the buyer.

At first, the buyer's response was limited to a "thank you." After two weeks, he suggested she schedule a phone call at week's end. Then it transitioned to a conference with other specialists and stakeholders.

Our friend, the VP of Sales, admitted that he was getting concerned. She was eating up resources and taking technical specialists away from their normal duties. Every Monday she was on a plane to one of their facilities or another. He feared that she would never meet her quota if she devoted all of her time to this one opportunity.

So, how did the story turn out? Our seller's quota was $5M for the year. She sold $6M in year one, $13M in year two, and $4M in year three of the contract the buying organization signed.

The buyer explained that "to make the change, I had to find someone who would immerse herself in the options and implications of the choices facing us. I needed someone who was above the politics and grounded in the numbers. When she sent me the first weekly update, I knew we had the right person. We needed a 'game changer,' not a drive-by seller."

The tortoise often relies on a buyer-centric sales discovery process that guides the customer down the path that he/she must travel.

Deb Calvert stresses that questions are an effective means for sellers to *connect* with a stakeholder.[2] It's not just the question that forges the connection, it's what the question does to the stakeholder as he or she ponders a response. The question also energizes an emotional connection as the buyer recognizes that the seller cares enough to attempt discovering the needs of the buyer and offering a solution that addresses those needs.

---

## The Challenge of Buyer-Centered Selling

*The Buyer's Dilemma:* **Many buyers are faced with complex, enterprise-wide buying decisions that have made them fearful of becoming lost among several choices that seem identical and obstacles that seem insurmountable.** Where should they turn for guidance? Many buyers are looking for a "consultant" or "change agent" who can conduct a discovery process that captures relevant data and feedback. They want an activist who can bring stakeholders together to build consensus.

*The Seller's Challenge:* **Seller becomes "buyer centered" when they act as the consultant, guide, or mapmaker who aids the buyer in navigating the financial, operational, and political obstacles that often derail change.** Through an effective sales discovery process, sellers can help buyers understand their needs and anticipate barriers to change.

---

In this chapter, we take a close look at sales discovery, what can be gained by sellers and buyers, and the core elements of a discovery process and then take a deeper dive into how questions can be used to probe and explore the buyer's interests.

## WHAT IS SALES DISCOVERY?

"Discovery is about learning what your client needs, their strategic initiatives, their goals, and their outcomes. Discovery work is what allows you to neatly tie anything you propose to what your client needs and to tailor it to those specific needs."[3]

We offer a different definition that covers some of the same ground but takes a different twist. Sales discovery is a seller-led, buyer-endorsed

> Sales discovery is a seller-led, buyer-endorsed inquiry designed to assess an organization's readiness to change.

inquiry designed to assess an organization's readiness to change. Sales discovery is a two-way street that benefits both the seller and the buyer. It must be based upon collaboration and mutual disclosure. At its best, discovery is a give-and-take, working for both buyer and seller. Don't think of discovery as a "stage" in selling or buying. It is a continuous process that unites buyers, stakeholders, and sellers in focused, problem-solving discussions throughout the entire buying process.

The role, functions, and focus of sales discovery can differ from market to market and industry to industry. Some discovery processes may include a single seller and two or three stakeholders, while others may involve stakeholders located on different continents.

In many cases, the discovery process falls to a single seller. In other instances, the account size and complexity may require a team of specialists and sellers. Whatever the size or complexity, there is a significant payoff for both buyer and seller.

In the early stages of Jobs to Be Done (JTBD), sales discovery focuses on three key topics:

- Does the buyer have a Problem, Opportunity, or Threat (POT) that the seller can address?
- Does the buyer acknowledge that a Problem, Opportunity, or Threat (POT) exists and they want to do something about it? In other words, status quo is not the desired state.
- Is the buyer willing to dedicate resources to work with us on solving the POT? The buyer must put some skin in the game to show they are serious. Sellers don't need "tire kickers."

In the middle and later stages of the JTBD, sales discovery is focused on ensuring "nothing has changed" and looking for additional unknowns that could strengthen, stall, or derail the sales opportunity.

## What's in It for the Buyer?

For the right buyer—one facing significant internal and external challenges—the offer of a seller-led sales discovery process may seem like a "lifeline" to a sinking boat. Among many benefits, a sales discovery process can:

- Confirm or challenge the buyer's assumptions about the best course of action.
- Identify sources of risk that the buyer may have overlooked.
- Acquire an experienced guide and mapmaker who can help the buyer navigate a treacherous roadway.
- Gauge support among other users or stakeholders for any course of action.
- Determine to what degree the current supplier is well entrenched and supported.
- Assess the urgency and appetite for change among stakeholders.
- Map a course of planning, action, and evaluation.
- Help the buyer grasp the shortcomings of previous solutions.
- Benchmark past performance against test results from current trials.

## What's in It for the Seller?

Discovery processes can become a trove of opportunities for any seller willing to invest the time and effort to develop a long-term relationship by serving the interests of a prospective customer. Consider several of the many business benefits that can result from a discovery process that takes care of the buyer:

- A sound footing for qualifying the sales opportunity and assessing how key buying personnel will perform as business partners.
- A richer and deeper buyer engagement built upon credibility and trust.
- Evidence that when the seller keeps the buyer's issues at the forefront of their actions, it's a clear foundation for trust.[4]

- "A far better chance of offering a solution that will truly help the buyer" and connect the buyer's needs to the capabilities provided by the seller's solution.[5]
- A fuller understanding of the buyer's issues, the implications, and what the organization values. This insight becomes a foundation for conversations that are far and above what competitors offer.
- An opportunity to gauge the competitive landscape and gain a close read on the status of your solution versus the competition.
- An opportunity to connect with potential supporters and champions.
- An opportunity to "neutralize" the position of those advocating the status quo.

Buyer-centered sellers conduct a thorough discovery process and then share their "findings" with the stakeholders before they make a recommendation. This process allows the stakeholders to align on the findings or in some cases embellish or correct the findings. The result is consensus on the findings and the basis for a winning sales strategy.

## Four Agreements Essential to a Sales Discovery Process

Unlike smaller discovery efforts, large-scale or enterprise-wide discovery processes need limitations and guidelines. Buyers may want some assurance that the process will yield the most useful information in the shortest time. For larger discovery processes, four "agreements" may be necessary for the probing, polling, and problem-solving essential to create a compelling buyer-centric deliverable.

1. What is the common objective and scope of discovery?
2. What is the agreed-upon deliverable and timeframe?
3. How can we ensure the sharing of personal and business concerns by relevant stakeholders?
4. Who must we enlist to gain the best feedback and support?

## QUESTIONS THAT LEAVE THEIR MARK

The most challenging aspects of discovery lie in selecting, wording, timing and sequencing questions that, while buyer-centric, enable the seller to detect needs and connect solutions. Yet many sellers ask questions that, no matter how pointed and challenging they appear from the seller's perspective, amount to little more than, "How are things going?" Or, "Is there anything you want to tell me?"

Our point is that discovery requires careful planning to move the conversation in a direction that will benefit both parties. "If you don't know where you are going, no question will get you there."

Mike Kunkle points out that sellers need a plan for each interview or conversation. What is the seller attempting to uncover, and which approaches and questions are likely to help the seller uncover the buyer's needs?[6]

This means planning a strategy for uncovering needs that helps the interviewee realize the problem, its implications, and options for addressing the situation. Kunkle stresses that effective sales discovery processes pursue a common goal: help the stakeholder identify implications or outcomes of their current situation and establish a connection between the seller's solution and key business objectives.[7]

There are numerous systems that categorize discovery questions, including ones by Deb Calvert *(DISCOVER Questions™)*, Neil Rackham *(SPIN Selling)*, Bob Miller and Steve Heiman *(Conceptual Selling)*, and Mike Kunkle.

In Figures 3-1 and 3-2, we've included examples of discovery questions designed to guide the conversation toward describing the current state and a future state. The "current state" refers to the status quo or current conditions. The "future state" is a reference to conditions as the interviewee imagines post-implementation.

## Current State

| Question Type | Purpose | Example |
| --- | --- | --- |
| Problem, Opportunity, or Threat (POT) | Uncover a condition that threatens to adversely impact business activity | "You're looking at a significant supply chain issue. How will you insure timely delivery of parts and materials?" |
| Size | Determine the magnitude of the POT | "How far behind your production quotas have you fallen?" |
| Scope | Identify the stakeholders affected by the POT | "Besides you, who else in the organization is affected directly or indirectly by the POT?" |
| Implication | Determine the business and personal implications for the stakeholders | "What's the effect of the growing product failure rate on new account sales, and how has this affected you and the company?" |
| Cause | Determine the reason for the POT | "In your opinion, why is this happening." |
| Urgency | Identify the willingness to act | "How important is it to take corrective action immediately?" |

Figure 3-1: Probing Problems and Implications: Current State

## Future State

| Question Type | Purpose | Example |
| --- | --- | --- |
| Prioritize | To determine what initiative requires immediate action | "When you look at these three problem areas separately, which challenge stands out from the rest as requiring immediate action?" |
| Obstacles | Identify what stands in the way of solving the POT | "Sometimes one issue is plagued by more obstacles than the others. Which problem is going to be the biggest challenge for your team?" |
| Mindset | Determine who within the organization wants to act | "What direction do you personally endorse?" |
| Preference | Determine which solution will be endorsed | "When you compare our product to your current product/supplier, is there any reason you would not select us?" |
| Cost of Inaction | Determine the cost of doing nothing | "Do you agree with our calculation that the cost of inaction exceeds the cost of change?" |
| Decision | Ask for the business | "Are you comfortable moving ahead with us?" |

Figure 3-2: Probing Problems and Implications: Future State

## DESIGNING A SALES DISCOVERY PROCESS

### Get Started

- Know what information you need to gather to conduct the selling process. What kind of discovery process will best serve a sales opportunity of this size, scope, and timeframe? Does this opportunity warrant an exhaustive discovery process? Or, is this an instance in which the buyer has a committed course of action and requires (and wants) less involvement from the selling organization?
- Ask for permission, and determine what information would benefit the buying organization. What is the deliverable for the buyer? What obstacles may obstruct the process?
- Early in the discovery process, buyer-centered sellers focus on uncovering problems, opportunities, and threats as seen through the eyes of the buyers and stakeholders. Who sees a problem or threat that others have overlooked? Who is driven by urgency? Who is shouldering the ownership?
- Determine where the stakeholders are in the buying process. What questions, topics, or information will be valuable? Develop a mix of buyer-centered and seller-serving questions. Too many self-serving questions will send the wrong kind of message. Avoid questions that are answered from quick internet searches.

### Plan Interviews

You plan sales calls, don't you? The same rule applies when interviewing a stakeholder. It's a sales call!

- If helpful, choose a discovery or conversation "model." There are lots of options. Each has its strengths and limitations.
- Structure your conversations around key objectives such as the impact of the problem, opportunity, or threat. Who is adversely affected by the situation?
- Who is ignoring the problem, opportunity, or threat? Who welcomes change, and who is reluctant to change?

- Explore the size and scope of the problem, threat, or opportunity. What's the cause of the POT? What solutions were tried? How did they perform? Why did they fail? What measure defines success?

- Personalize questions for each stakeholder based upon their position and expertise. Listen for answers on key questions. Make sure you record quotes to share with the Executive Buyer and other pertinent stakeholders.

- Don't forget qualifying questions. It's vital that sellers continue to assess whether this is a good business deal with a good partner.

- In the latter stages of discovery, sellers may find it useful to formulate several hypotheses and raise them in a question format to test the efficacy of the potential relationship.

- Update the Executive Buyer and other pertinent stakeholders periodically with notes that highlight overall progress.

## Interview Guidelines

As you plan your interviews, keep the following guidelines in mind.

- Avoid asking too many questions. Remember that you are only "filling in the gaps" in your research. Conduct your research. Fill in as many gaps as you can before the discovery call.

- Know the link you want to create among the problem, its implications, and your product. This will help you formulate questions that take you in the right direction. Otherwise the buyer may drift toward a problem that is unrelated to your product.

- Always drill down on a problem, threat, or opportunity. This is your chance to gain a complete understanding of the implications (size, scope, urgency) and its cause.

- Mission critical is to help the buyer see a connection between the future state and the current state. The larger the gap, the easier it will be to accept your solution.

- In a discovery call, you may need to spend some time and effort uncovering more than one problem or threat. Remember that you have a "deliverable" that you promised to the Executive Buyer or other pertinent stakeholders. How has this discovery call helped prepare you to provide that deliverable?

- Expect your stakeholders to drift from one concern to another. Your challenge may become a time-management issue. Often the drift means the problem is overly broad, with many implications.

## INSIGHT TOOLS THAT ENRICH THE SALES DISCOVERY PROCESS

From the outside looking in, discovery appears to be nothing more than well-planned interviews driven by probing questions. If that were all, it would be better than what many sellers are doing today. For some sellers, the interviews are self-serving questions that "fill in" the seller's blind spots and provide little value to the buyer. But these sessions are not just interviews—they are work sessions in which stakeholders join with sellers to explore concerns, needs, sources of pain, implications, assumptions about cause and effect, prospects for the future, the impact of needs unaddressed, future expectations, and resource and alignment issues.

There are times when these sessions require greater detail than can be gained through questions alone. Consider some of the "tools" used by top performers to clarify responses to questions:

Figure 3-3: Sales Discovery Tools Used by Top Performers

**Collaborative Planning.** Often buyers and sellers find themselves working at odds. The buyer is pursuing the best deal while overcoming internal obstacles within their own organization. The seller is attempting to build a support base committed to selecting their product or service. A collaborative planning document connects the seller and buyer through a "buyer-focused" strategy.

**Brainstorming.** Some sellers find brainstorming useful in exploring "what if" scenarios with stakeholders, sketching timelines and ranking the order of preferences. Brainstorming can help in mapping a future course of action that fuels the buying process.

**Surveys & Polling.** Top performers recognize that buyers are interested in how ideas (options) are received by others in the organization—especially users who are outside the buying process. Surveys and polls provide quick responses to options and arm stakeholders with a quick read on the work that needs to be accomplished to build support for an option.

**Business Case.** Few sellers get excited by the prospect of having to create a business case for their product or solution. However, most top performers understand that a well-written business case can be a powerful "proof of claim." If Procurement is involved, it may be wise to collaborate and share data.

**Mind Mapping.** Mind mapping is a great tool for showing relationships. If the seller is exploring the business outcomes resulting from a change (merger, expansions, reorganization, etc.), a mind map can help capture the visual relationships under discussion.

**Presentation of Findings.** Prior to providing a solution or recommendation, its often useful to provide a presentation of your findings. This allows the seller to receive affirmation that they understood the POT thoroughly and to receive feedback before they provide their recommendations. Oftentimes, buyers will provide additional key information at this time, including preferences and priorities.

## Key Points to Remember for Buyer-Centered Sellers

Consider these insights and observations when building a discovery process.

1. Sales discovery is a buyer-led, buyer-endorsed inquiry designed to access an organization's readiness to change.

2. Improving sales discovery skills is key to increasing overall sales productivity.

3. Your buyer may be facing complex, enterprise-wide decisions and wondering where to turn for help.

4. Buyers can benefit from a third-party assessment of the situation.

5. Sellers can help buyers uncover overlooked sources of risk that jeopardize the status quo.

6. Sellers can help buyers assess the desire for change among stakeholders.

7. A sales discovery process can help the seller qualify an opportunity, problem, or threat.

8. Buyer and seller must agree upon a common objective, a deliverable for the buyer and seller, and a responsible timeline.

9. Good discovery requires careful planning and rehearsal.

10. Discovery is not a discrete step in the sales process. It is a continuous activity.

11. In the middle and later stages of the JTBD, sales discovery is focused on ensuring "nothing has changed" and looking for additional unknowns that could strengthen, stall, or derail the sales opportunity.

12. Sales discovery helps the buyer recognize unseen outcomes or implications from their failure to act or change.

13. Sales discovery helps the seller establish a link between the product/solution and the resolution of buyer problems or threats.

## THE SKILL CHALLENGE

In order to become more effective and buyer centered, what is the one thing you will commit to do differently because of reading this chapter? Please write it here or on a separate sheet of paper.

---

---

---

## ADDENDUM 8: COLLABORATION PLAN

The Collaboration Plan (CP) is a plan between the buying and selling organizations to explore jointly the feasibility and benefit of a partnership. It's a sharing of ideas, concerns, capabilities and obstacles that must be addressed and overcome in formalizing an agreement. The CP guides the buyer and seller through a complex decision process that otherwise might be delayed, stalled or set aside. From the seller's perspective, the CP keeps selling activities "buyer-focused" and connected to the needs of the customer. For the buyer's position, the CP ensures joint efforts to navigate hurdles and barriers and ensure that the buying organization is "change ready."

### Collaboration Plan
(Between Customer and Supplier)

| JTBD Description (Brief description of project) | Process Manager |
| --- | --- |
| | Sales Rep |

**Commitments Required and Agreed to:** (Please check each box as appropriate)

| | | | |
| --- | --- | --- | --- |
| ☐ Time | ☐ Collaboration | ☐ Review | ☐ Execute |
| ☐ Exploration | ☐ Build Consensus | ☐ Resolve Concerns | ☐ Evaluate |
| ☐ Change | ☐ Invest | ☐ Decision | |

**Gap Analysis** (Please be specific)

| Current State | Future State | Cost of Inaction |
| --- | --- | --- |
| (What is the problem, opportunity or threat?) Quantify it! | (What is the desired change?) | Revenue/Cost/Risk Impact |
| | | Stakeholder(s) Impacted |
| | | Organizational Unit Impacted |

**Barriers to Change** (Please check appropriate box and explain in detail below)

| ☐ Mitigate Risk | ☐ Clarify Funding | ☐ Build Support | ☐ Other |
| --- | --- | --- | --- |
| | | | |

| Priority & Urgency (Please explain in detail) | Time Frame and Results (Please enter appropriate dates) | |
| --- | --- | --- |
| On a scale of 0 to 10 with 10 being the highest, how important is this initiative to your organization? _____ | Project Start Date | (dd/mm/yy) |
| | Formalize Action Plan | (dd/mm/yy) |
| What is the cause of the Problem, Opportunity or Threat (POT)? | Action Plan Review Schedule | (dd/mm/yy) |
| | Formal Agreement | (dd/mm/yy) |
| Why does the POT need to be addressed now? | Implementation Start | (dd/mm/yy) |
| | Go Live | (dd/mm/yy) |
| | Financial Benefits Achieved By Customer | (dd/mm/yy) |

# Chapter 4

# From Jekyll to Hyde: Selling to a Buyer's Behavioral Style

"82% of buyers make deals with salespeople who match or effectively mirror their personality style."

Gil Cargill—President, *Cargill Consulting Group*

For centuries, sellers—those of us who peddle, barter, and trade for a living—have struggled to understand what makes our customers tick. Why are some buyers demanding, analytic, and detailed oriented while others are engaging, tolerant, and supportive? How can we predict, understand, and adapt to their differences?

## WHO IS YOUR BUYER?

It is vital for us to understand how people behave when they converse, buy, and decide. Research shows a lineage of behavioral styles, personas, social styles, personality types, and mindsets. Some of this research has been driven by an interest in social interaction, while other scholarship has focused on executive behavior, customer service, or a general understanding of different learning styles.

So many disciplines—sales, marketing, interpersonal communication, industrial psychology, and learning theory—have a stake in understanding how people behave. Each discipline uses behavioral styles to answer fundamental questions and unlock both descriptive and predictive models of behavior. Jeb Blount argues that sellers need to deploy a style that engages and connects with the buyer's emotional levers.[1]

In the late 1950s, Eric Berne outlined three "ego states" that help us understand how people relate in a social context. It was popularized in the book *Games People Play.*[2]

In 2005, Bob Miller and Gary Williams published *The 5 Paths to Persuasion,* a seminal work that focused on five "styles" of executives.[3] Their research included 1,700 key executives and identified 5 executive mindsets. Their research helped them answer several fundamental questions about executive styles. What draws the attention of executives? How do executives prefer to consume information? How do executives learn?

Cathcart and Allessandra, two well-known researchers, developed a classification system of communication styles that included Thinkers, Directors, Relators, and Socializers.[4]

The most widely used of all these behavioral systems is DiSC®, developed by Walter Clark Associates in 1956 (and based upon the research and theory of William Marston in the late 1920s). DiSC® identifies 4 styles that underlie behavior. Identified as "behavioral style," Clark's work and subsequent research in industrial psychology have served as a foundation to our understanding of how people conduct business and exchange information in an interactive work environment.[5]

We are huge believers in using Behavioral Style Assessments in business to improve productivity and communication. When used with sales teams, they help sales professionals communicate more effectively with their prospects, their customers, management, and support personnel.

The simple fact that people buy from people they like is still true. Stakeholders tend to like, be attracted to, and be more trusting of people who are like them. Sales professionals build credibility and trust when they adapt their behavioral style in a manner that complements the style of the person they are talking to. This causes the other person to be more willing to engage in a meaningful conversation. Each of us has a unique manner. Some of us are direct and forceful, while some of us are outgoing and accommodating. Others are data driven and methodical, or courteous and reflective. There is no right or wrong behavioral style. It is simply a reflection of who we are. Once we recognize another individual's behavioral style, it is easy to adapt to their style and build rapport with them.

In this chapter, we explore the types of behavioral styles.

## What Is a Behavioral Style?

A behavioral or communication style denotes a preferred manner of behavior. It's a person's default mode for sending and receiving information and relating to others. Some people prefer detail and elaboration. Others focus on highlights and headline banners. Some prefer change and novelty. Many are skeptical and challenging.

> A behavioral or communication style denotes a preferred manner of behavior. It's a person's default mode for sending and receiving information and relating to others.

One lesson we have learned from volumes of research and literature is that understanding how others prefer to receive information allows us to adapt and gain a distinct advantage when conveying our content. Knowing how others like to receive information solves the Jekyll versus Hyde dilemma. Consider the combination of Jekylls and Hydes in this story of a trade show seller.

### Story: Selling a Trade Show Exhibit

Tim Johnson is a sales representative for Revolutionary Display & Exhibits. His firm is the worldwide market leader, providing a single source of innovative, high quality trade show display products, portable exhibits, booths, and banner stands to organizations worldwide.

For the last few months, Tim has been calling on Bronson Software about the design and purchase of a new trade show booth for the largest convention in their industry, which will be in eight months. To meet this timetable, a decision needs to be made in the next two weeks. Tim has a meeting scheduled in two days with the following company representatives from Bronson Software:

- o　Jennifer Abrams: Trade Show Coordinator
- o　Lisa Willis: Director of Marketing
- o　John Hollon: Chief Financial Officer
- o　Mike Smith: Vice President of Sales

Because the meeting is so important, Tim reviewed his call plan with Steve Perry, his Regional Sales Manager, who will accompany him on this call. In a telephone call with Steve, Tim described each person as follows:

Jennifer Abrams (Trade Show Coordinator) is an outgoing bubble of energy. You will love her personality. She has been very helpful in getting me the information I need to provide a creative solution within budget. When you meet her, don't rush her. She likes to talk. This is why I want to arrive early.

Lisa Willis (Director of Marketing) is the opposite of Jennifer. She is quiet and reserved. She asks a lot of questions and wants input from everyone who is involved in the decision about whether to use our firm. She is cautious, and if everyone wasn't being pushed by the VP of Sales to get a new larger, more contemporary trade show booth, she would be happy to stay with their existing booth.

John Hollon (Chief Financial Officer) focuses on the details. He has scrutinized our proposed costs and asked for an explanation of every line item. He has also asked me to provide him with six references he could call.

Mike Smith (Vice President of Sales) is a no-nonsense guy. He wants this project decided quickly. Yesterday, on a call with Lisa and myself, he told her to make a recommendation to him, or he would decide himself.

As you read through this chapter, see if you can determine the behavioral style of each person. At the end of the chapter, we will provide the answers.

---

## The Challenge of Buyer-Centered Selling

*The Buyer's Dilemma:* **With very little time and many decisions facing stakeholders, the dilemma lies in determining who to trust, who is a viable source of service, and who can provide valued information in a form that can be easily processed.** Do some sellers appear too distant or inquiring or detailed? Who really cares about the issues that concern us most? To what extent am I willing to share our vulnerabilities, competitive threats, and business concerns? Outside of a product or service, who can I trust to work collaboratively on our behalf?

*The Seller's Challenge:* **The challenge facing many sellers is to better understand how a buyer wishes to consume information vital to a purchasing decision. To build trust and communicate effectively, sellers must understand the behavioral styles of prospects, customers, and influencers.** To be buyer-centered means adapting the seller's message and mannerisms to the way stakeholders prefer to consume ideas, data, and advice.

---

Everyone is a blend of the 4 behavioral styles (Figure 4-1). The styles do not identify abilities or personalities; they demonstrate a person's priorities and preferences on the Behavioral Style Model. No one style is better than another.

Figure 4-1 shows the characteristics that determine where an individual might fall on a generic Behavioral Model. Our generic model includes 4 behavioral styles: Driver, Socializer, Supportive, and Thinker. To determine whether someone is a Driver, a Socializer, a Supportive, or a Thinker, sellers must begin by asking if this person is "Direct & Forceful," or more "Out-Going & Relationship-Oriented," "Accepting & Warm," or "Questioning & Data Driven."

Trained sellers can quickly infer a person's default style from a brief conversation (or by thinking about past conversations). The model helps to improve communication.

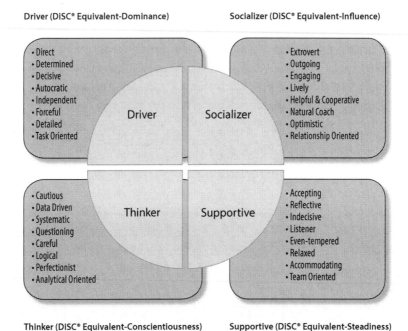

Figure 4-1: Behavioral Style Characteristics

## OVERVIEW OF THE FOUR BEHAVIORAL STYLES

DRIVER                    These individuals tend to be assertive, confident, and
                          bold. They do not have an issue expressing their point
                          of view. Individuals who fall in the Driver style know
                          what they want and will make up their minds quickly
                          once they have the facts. They have a take-charge atti-
                          tude, which may cause them to dominate conversations
                          with others. These people are direct, decisive, strong-
                          willed, and determined. They are action oriented, with
                          a philosophy of "Get it done." Drivers crave respect for
                          achievement. An example of someone with this style
                          is Donald Trump or Mark Cuban.

SOCIALIZER    Socializers tend to be extroverts, optimistic, and have high energy. They focus on building relationships, and they use their outgoing personality to influence others. They are more attracted to people who are fun and exciting versus those who are logical and practical. They crave social approval, so they are good at making everyone feel comfortable and welcome in meetings. An example of someone with this style would be Jay Leno or Oprah Winfrey.

SUPPORTIVE    Someone who has a Supportive style is very accommodating, soft-spoken, and humble. Even though they are friendly and appear to be agreeable, these individuals tend to be very careful when they decide; they almost appear reluctant. When it's time to commit, they will want to make sure the decision is the right one, before agreeing. Individuals who are Supportive avoid change at all costs and are reluctant to try a new way of doing things. They prefer the status quo until they are given a strong reason to change. They also avoid conflict if it arises, and they are people pleasers. They need consistency, predictability, and security. An example of someone with this style would be Mother Teresa or Diana, Princess of Wales.

THINKER    These individuals tend to be reserved, unemotional, analytical, and systematic. Before deciding, they will consider all their options. They are often very quiet; they do not come off as energetic. They simply stick to facts and do not engage in small talk with others. They can feel manipulated if a salesperson asks too many personal questions. A person with this style will base their decision on objective information rather than emotion or intuition. Their greatest fear is being wrong. An example of someone with this style would be Albert Einstein or Bill Gates.

Individuals who fall into the "Driver" or "Thinker" categories are detail oriented. Those who fall into the "Socializer" or "Supportive" categories are people oriented.

## HOW THE SELLER CAN ADAPT TO EACH BEHAVIORAL STYLE

Since everyone has a different personality or behavioral style, sellers must adapt their selling approach to meet the needs of individual buyers. This requires them to think carefully about how they will interact, ask questions, and provide information.

### Buyer-Centered Selling to the Driver Style

Because Drivers make decisions quickly, you must not challenge them. Let them have control. They expect it and require it. If you challenge them, they will eat your lunch and then throw you to the wolves.

Earn their respect by being confident in your ability to get things done. Be brief and concise when answering their questions. Always meet their timelines. Drivers will challenge you to see if you will cower. Don't be intimidated, and do not act scared or weak. This is especially true during negotiations. Don't cower! Instead, stand up to them in a respectful manner, and exude confidence in your ability. Negotiate for a win-win relationship.

To develop a relationship with a Driver, demonstrate competence and confidence. They like sales professionals who are brief, prepared, and then gone. Communicate using bullets and short, concise sentences. Don't waste their time, or they will lose respect for you.

## Buyer-Centered Selling to the Socializer Style

Selling to this style is the easiest for sellers because they are easy to approach and engage, and they are open to building relationships. These buyers will have a positive outlook and a fast, action-oriented pace. They are willing to try innovative options, and they care about others' feelings.

Socializers are the individuals who talk incessantly and can often ramble. They tell elaborate stories and are not afraid to express their opinion or provide the "inside scoop." This makes them an excellent candidate to become an influencer and develop into a sponsor if they like your product, service, or solution. Because they enjoy being the center of attention, they crave compliments and flattery and fear rejection.

Selling to Socializers takes time. You must let them talk and not interrupt them. They are eternal optimists. Thus, it may take more sales calls to accomplish your goals with a Socializer. Be patient; they will buy from you and continue to buy from you because you listen to them. A meeting agenda will help to keep them focused.

## Buyer-Centered Selling to the Supportive Style

Individuals that fall under the Supportive style are risk averse. They like to please people and will not decide unless they are sure of the outcomes. They have an agreeable demeanor, are soft spoken, exhibit patient listening skills, are reluctant to commit quickly, and do not like change. Because they crave certainty, they avoid risk, and they tend to move at a slow, methodical pace. These individuals cannot be rushed.

Sellers must match their slow pace and be very patient not to push them. When pushed, the Supportive style simply shuts down to you and your ideas, and you may never know it, but behind the scenes, they could become your anti-sponsor.

Supportive style individuals are very good listeners. They will allow a sales professional to bury themselves by becoming a talking leaflet. These individuals are unlikely to make a commitment unless they feel they can fully trust a person. Approaching this style must come off as genuine and thoughtful.

## Buyer-Centered Selling to the Thinker Style

The Thinker style wants to make the correct decision. They abhor mistakes. They ask sellers for detailed information to ensure they can make an informed, intelligent decision.

The Thinker style is a stickler for detail. They will check every fact, figure, and number for accuracy and completeness. They also tend to over-analyze and may seem to be overly critical. Because they are very private, they often appear to be aloof and non-communicative. Often, they won't return telephone calls or emails unless they concern something they need.

Thinkers request data and proof. Sellers should be prepared to provide the science behind their algorithms, case studies, testimonials, references, published literature, etc. When providing the information, make it interactive, and be brief and relevant. Sales professionals must draw the Thinker's style into the conversation. These individuals emphasize quality, competence, dependability, and information.

## DO'S & DON'TS OF EACH BEHAVIORAL STYLE

Knowing which selling behaviors are effective with each behavioral style can be challenging. Consider these "do's" and "don'ts" as you build your sales approach.

| Do's | | | |
|------|------|------|------|
| **Driver**<br>DiSC®=Dominance | **Socializer**<br>DiSC®= Influence | **Supportive**<br>DiSC®= Steadiness | **Thinker**<br>DiSC®= Conscientiousness |
| Be Confident | Greet Them Warmly | Be Calm & Patient | Provide Proof |
| Let Them Be in Control | Listen & Don't Interrupt | Ask Questions to Understand Risks | Be Organized & On-Time |
| Be Punctual | Compliment Them | Be Tactful | Conduct Research Before the Meeting |
| Exhibit Confidence & Competence | Be Out-Going | Be Non-Threatening | Provide Facts, Figures & Numbers |
| Be Succinct, Clear & Specific | Let Them Talk About Themselves | Be Genuine & Thoughtful | Be Accurate & Precise |

| Do's | | | |
|---|---|---|---|
| **Driver** DiSC°=Dominance | **Socializer** DiSC°= Influence | **Supportive** DiSC°= Steadiness | **Thinker** DiSC°= Conscientiousness |
| Use Bullets in PowerPoint | Let Them State Their Opinion | Position Yourself as a Team Player | Be Polite |
| Discuss Outcomes | Show Interest in Their Personal Hobbies | Provide Clear Guidelines | Follow Up Every Meeting |
| Be Prepared | Discuss Emotions and Feelings | Provide Them with Options | Be Brief & Relevant |

Figure 4-2: Behavioral Style Do's

| Don'ts | | | |
|---|---|---|---|
| **Driver** DiSC°=Dominance | **Socializer** DiSC°= Influencer | **Supportive** DiSC°= Steadiness | **Thinker** DiSC°= Conscientiousness |
| Don't Challenge Them | Don't Argue with Them | Don't Be Pushy or Aggressive | Don't Appear Disorganized |
| Don't Cower | Don't Appear Aloof or Cold | Don't Overly Compliment Them | Don't Allow Mistakes in Your Work |
| Don't Waste Their Time | Don't Get into Facts, Figures, & Numbers | Don't Try to Move Too Fast | Don't Jump from Topic to Topic |
| Don't Be Disorganized | Don't Compete with Them for Talk Time | Don't Speak in a Forceful Tone | Don't Try to Develop a Personal Relationship |
| Don't Discuss Features & Benefits | Don't Appear Hurried | Don't Expect a Quick Decision | Don't Be Emotional |
| Don't Act Weak or Scared | Don't Tune Them Out When They are Talking | Don't be Ambiguous with Your Requests | Don't Come Unprepared |
| Don't Be Late | Don't Be Overly Analytical | Don't Place Them in a Situation with Conflict | Don't Tell Them They Are Wrong |

Figure 4-3: Behavioral Style Don'ts

As you can see, understanding your own behavioral style and that of your prospects, customers, counterparts, manager, spouse, significant others, children, and friends is relatively easy with a little training.

**Answers to the Story**

Now let's take a review of which characters in our story match up to specific behavioral styles. See if you agree with our analysis.

Jennifer Abrams is a Socializer.

Lisa Willis is a Supportive.

John Hollon is a Thinker.

Mike Smith is a Driver.

In the last few pages, we have provided a primer using a generic Behavioral Style Model. The profile we recommend, use, and sell in our business is EVERYTHING DiSC,® a Wiley Brand. It is the most trusted behavioral profiling instrument in the industry and is used by millions of training and coaching professionals around the globe.

Readers who wish to explore the DiSC® concept more fully should go to our website www.strategicdynamicsfirm.com/assessments/everything-DiSC to learn more, order an assessment, or obtain some of our additional resources.

**Key Points to Remember for Buyer-Centered Sellers**

Once a seller understands the Behavioral Style Model, they can use it to be more effective by:

1. Recognizing there are four different behavioral styles for every stakeholder and that sometimes behavior can be a blend of two styles.
2. Having a clear understanding of each buyer's behavioral style.
3. Drivers are assertive, confident, bold, and controlling. They expect confidence in a seller. But don't challenge the Driver.
4. Socializers are extroverted, high energy relationship builders. Sellers should let them carry the conversation and respond with warmth, humor, compliments, and genuine interest.
5. Supportives are accommodative, easy going, friendly, and agreeable. In turn, sellers should be calm, patient, and non-threatening.
6. Thinkers are interested in your plan, not you. They care about details, logic, and step-wise progressions. The solution must survive careful

scrutiny. As a seller, avoid mistakes in logic or data analysis. Be prepared to take them on a step-by-step journey through your thought process.

7. Sellers should quickly assess each buyer's style and how each stakeholder wishes to receive and consume information.

8. Sellers should adjust their behavior to match the buyer's style more effectively. Often this means the seller must leave their comfort zone and adapt to the dominant style of the Executive Buyer.

9. No one behavioral style is better than another.

## THE SKILL CHALLENGE

In order to become more effective and buyer centered, what skill can you identify from the content in this chapter that requires skill and practice? Please write it here or on a separate sheet of paper.

_____

_____

_____

_____

_____

_____

_____

_____

_____

_____

_____

_____

_____

# Chapter 5

# Differentiating with Value Messages That Snap, Crackle and Pop!

"Stop talking about yourself and your company and begin leading with the issues, pains, problems, opportunities and results that are important to your prospect."

Mike Weinberg—Author of *Sales Simplified*

We all know what constitutes a value proposition or statement. It's a concise, clear, and compelling message that conveys the benefit a product, service, or solution provides the buyer's organization. In other words, it's a promise or pledge made by the seller to convey value to the buyer. But this is where our understanding gets clouded. There is a difference between marketing's version of a value proposition and the flexibility required by sales representatives meeting with different buyers at several levels of target organizations. Neither is wrong—just different.

Often marketing is focused on a single message that draws attention and can serve as a platform for the buyer-seller discussion. However, the sales team is focused on differentiating their solution from competitor offerings and internal default options often thought of as the "status quo" or "current state." Sales representatives don't need a slogan, motto, or infomercial. They are looking to marry insight into their customer's needs with product capabilities that resonate as compelling and documentable solutions that stand apart from other viable alternatives. When asked, we define a value proposition as a promise made by a selling organization of the tangible (usually business) results accruing to a buyer from purchasing the seller's product or services. Compelling value propositions will use their claim to differentiate their product from the competition and offer proof for their claim.[1]

> A value proposition is a promise made by a selling organization of the tangible (usually business) results accruing to a buyer from purchasing the seller's product or services.

Don't think of a value proposition as a sentence or two that can be dusted off and rolled out for any buyer. Imagine you are growing a "tree" with each limb slightly different from the next. The lower limbs are focused on technical buyers. The middle limbs are pruned for department heads, supervisors, and daily users of the solution. The upper growth reflects the needs and values of senior buyers and executives. Perhaps the trunk of the tree is the broad-based, enterprise-level value proposition that is amplified on your website, in product literature, advertising, etc.

## Story: One Size Doesn't Fit All Stakeholders

Here is a simple example of a value proposition that has gone awry because it is specific to only one stakeholder. Imagine that you are the seller of a da Vinci robot! To the seller, it's a robotic device in the healthcare industry that helps the surgeon improve the quality and precision of their work. This generic value message, however, won't resonate with non-surgeon stakeholders. Sellers must adapt it as follows to resonate with each different stakeholder, depending on their role and responsibility.

- *For the Patient ...* it's space-age technology that offers the hope of less pain, quicker recovery, and a better clinical outcome.
- *For the Operating Room Director or Clinical Service Line Director ...* it's technology that will impact the workflow and productivity of the department in a positive and measurable way.
- *For a Vice President of Procurement ...* it's an opportunity to reduce procedure costs significantly while enhancing their value to the CEO.
- *For the CFO ...* it's a capital expenditure and investment in technology to drive revenue and market share by attracting new patients.
- *For the CEO/COO ...* it's an investment in technology to keep the physicians happy and improve patient outcomes. It's also a way to show the Governing Board that they are executing the vision and strategy of the hospital to be a technological leader in the community.
- *For the Governing Board* ... it's a way of positioning the hospital as providing the latest in cutting edge technology for improving patient care.

Lesson: Sellers must make sure they provide the right value propositions to the right stakeholder! Later in this chapter we share proven ways to make value statements more relevant to each stakeholder.

---

## The Challenge of Buyer-Centered Selling

*The Buyer's Dilemma:* **Faced with different messages of questionable credibility, buyers are challenged to differentiate solutions by assessing the veracity of claims, the relevance of capabilities to business outcomes, and concerns of risk.** In an effort to resolve their dilemma, buyers often search outside their organization for assistance and guidance.

---

*The Seller's Challenge:* **Create value messages that bring into clear focus what's meaningful to buyers. Value messages must help differentiate the product as essential and unique and simplify the selection process.** As B2B selling becomes more complex, involving more stakeholders with different perspectives on the business and personal benefits of a solution, sellers are challenged with creating value messages and implementing communication plans that convey value for each buyer at every stage of the buying journey.

---

It may seem like a daunting task...but this is one of the most important functions sellers perform: they connect their product or solution to their customer's needs in ways that resonate and convey relevance, uniqueness, and urgency. Since different "personas" in the buying organization are charged with different responsibilities, sellers must become well versed in the broader landscape of values that each buyer brings to meetings, conversations, presentations, and phone calls.

In this chapter, we focus on customizing the content of value messages. Buyer-centered sellers create communication plans that are broad in reach and compelling in content.

## WHY CREATE VALUE MESSAGES?

It's easy to think of value messages as optional. After all, the meeting seemed to go well. The buying team appeared engaged. There were lots of smiles, and camaraderie was high. Consider what researchers are finding:

- Corporate Visions reports that sellers' failure to communicate value is the primary reason that sales representatives fall short of quota. Researchers explain that "if your sales force cannot communicate why your solution is different, better, and worth more, there is nothing your sales strategy can do to fix that."[2]
- When Sirius Decisions surveyed buying executives about the value of sales calls, approximately 90% of the respondents felt that sales calls failed to provide value that warranted the time invested in the call.[3]

Consider the case for crafting effective value messages as a centerpiece for your sales strategy. Compelling buyer-centered value messages:

- Create a persistent and recurring theme that gives focus to sales calls, meetings, conversations, presentations, emails, and phone calls.
- Provide "talking points" that engage the buyer.
- Educate and inform buyers, often opening eyes to a new perspective.
- Set the seller apart and advance the buying process.
- Keep the seller focused on what the product or solution does for the customer's organization.
- Provide the buyer a compelling alternative to price in justifying a decision to purchase their product or solution.
- Create a sense of urgency that will hasten the buying decision.

## What Does "Differentiation" Do?

This may be the easiest question raised in this chapter. As we look back over how differentiation is used and defined in other books, our colleagues have helped us out. There are three conditions that contribute to differentiation of a product, service, or solution: relevance, uniqueness, and urgency. Is the product or service relevant to corporate goals or vital initiatives? Otherwise, it may fall lower on the list of priorities. Is the product or service offered unique from other competitive offerings? In other words, does it claim to provide a service or a capability that others cannot rightfully claim? Otherwise, a buyer may be unable to differentiate one option from another. Is there an urgency to purchase this product at this time? If not, the buying process can become stalled or delayed.

Without differentiation, it becomes easy for a buyer to commoditize products as indistinguishable from one another. The buyer thinks, "Why should I pay more for a product that is indistinguishable from the others?" You've got it: without differentiation, the lowest price wins!

### What's a Commoditizer?

> Commoditizers are messages that are intended to sell your product but, in fact, fail to differentiate you, your company, or your product.

Commoditizers are messages that are intended to sell your product but, in fact, fail to differentiate you, your company, or your product.

There are four categories of commoditizers.

- **"Me too"** messages. "Our product can match the performance claims of any of our competitors."
- **"Cheap"** messages. "When you compare all the products in this category, you'll be shocked at how inexpensive our product is."
- **"Prideful"** messages. "It took 23 of the world's top hydraulic engineers almost 4 years to perfect the design of this product."
- **"Feature-focused"** messages. "This is our premier model, and it comes in your choice of 11 vibrant colors."

So, if you want to sell value instead of price, focus on how your product or service is relevant to vital business initiatives of the buyer, has qualities that other products lack, and warrants a timely purchase to realize immediate benefits. That's your differentiation! Then make sure you never find yourself making claims that others can easily duplicate.

## CREATE POWERFUL MESSAGES

When crafting a portfolio of value messages, consider how well your planned message addresses five questions that are gnawing at buyers as they consider their options.

- **Value Claim.** "How will this product benefit my organization, enabling me to address, resolve, or accomplish my needs?"
- **Differentiation.** "How unique and relevant are their benefits compared to our current solution or supplier?"
- **Proof.** "How do I know that this product will perform as promised?"
- **Risk.** "What steps has the supplier taken to minimize the risks if I adopt his/her solution? What is the risk if I don't adopt their solution?"
- **Urgency.** "How vital is it that I act now?" "Will I still gain the same benefit if I delay the purchase by one month or even six months?

### Five Steps in Crafting Value Messages That Are Buyer-Centered

Sellers may consider these five steps in designing their "value tree."

Figure 5-1: Five Steps in Crafting a Message

1. **Discover Your Customer's Needs.** Discover your customer's needs at three levels of the buying organization: technical specialists, users, and executives. Map all stakeholders in the buying process to one of the three levels. Identify their priorities. Explore how each stakeholder defines and measures the solution. Think about each of the four boxes below as possible limbs on a value tree. Sellers should use their conversations with stakeholders to prune and shape each limb.

   Revenue "limbs" are typically money or purchased resources that are hard to get and terrible to lose. They can take the form of Return on Investment (ROI), Internal Rate of Return (IRR), Net Present Value

(NPV), or Payback due to patents, proprietary technology, speed to market, speed of service, etc. Decreasing costs may be due to product standardization or cost reductions such as expense over-rides or unplanned training costs. Mitigating or Eliminating Risk may mean no system or production errors, minimal repair issues, or fear of job loss if the project doesn't deliver the desired results. Improving Efficiency or Productivity is often about time. It may be reducing churn, improving work flow, etc., or it may be about productivity, e.g., retaining talent, developing new skills, or effective onboarding of new recruits.

Figure 5-2: Four Limbs on a Value Tree

2. **Identify Customer's Benefits.** Identify a broad spectrum of potential benefits, including "soft benefits." While measurable benefits can be extremely helpful with the proper documentation, soft benefits may not appeal much to a technical specialist but may pique the interest of an executive. Sellers should use conversations with their customers to determine what value claims create the greatest traction. Robert Kaplan & David Norton provided a framework for discovering overlooked tangible benefits in their book *Strategy Maps: Converting Intangible Assets into Tangible Outcomes.*[4] Intangible assets are benefits

that impact organizational health and performance in a positive way, but are not easily measured, like recruiting a higher grade employee or shortening the training cycle for "users."

3. **Document Claims.** Explore how your current customers and users document product or solution value. Sellers should schedule phone calls and in-person visits with current customers and ask, "What measurable benefit have you received from our product?" It can be surprising to discover how customers prioritize, quantify, and document value.

4. **Customize Terminology.** Tailor the value statements to resonate with each buying "persona." Phrase each value statement using the language of the buying organization and stakeholder. Sometimes stakeholders will write their own value statement. Listen carefully to their responses to questions.

5. **Test Impact.** Sellers should test their value propositions with champions, current customers, and members of the sales team. Is the message compelling? Does it differentiate clearly and forcefully? Does it convey relevance, uniqueness and urgency? Can the claim, pledge or promise be proven?

Over time, sellers should continue to document, customize, and test the impact of the message.

## HOW BUYER-CENTERED SELLERS CRAFT VALUE MESSAGES

In working with sellers who are focused on helping buyers make their selection, we've identified guidelines they follow in creating and implementing value messages.

- Don't try to compose a single sentence to serve as a value message. Put together several sentences that work well together. In this way, you can add or subtract elements as appropriate. A value message is not a monologue—it's a brief twenty-second statement meant to arouse interest, prompt insight, and differentiate or advance the buying process.

- Prepare yourself to answer questions and concerns such as "What proof do you have?" "Who can attest to your claim?" "Don't your competitors have the same capability?" Remember: the point is to get buyers engaged and simplify selection.
- Refine value messages periodically. A customer's needs may change over time, and your value messages will benefit from a "refresh."
- Make sure all teammates are familiar with and well rehearsed in the options for conveying value at different levels of the organization.
- Share value messages used in deals that were WON and LOST across all sellers, no need to reinvent messages that may be compelling with customers in certain verticals, confronting the same issues, etc.

A vital learning point is that value messages are best developed by small groups of two or three sellers who can test and challenge each other in perfecting their messages.

## CHOOSE A MODEL THAT WORKS

It seems that every blog, article, or chapter in a book that mentions value propositions also includes a template for crafting a value statement. That's helpful until the seller begins to apply various formats only to discover that they don't fit, explain, or clarify the value of his/her product, service, or solution. Our recommendation is to stay away from the "fill in the blanks" templates and look more closely at formats that raise questions (for the seller to answer) or identify content characteristics that the seller should strive to achieve in the value statement. In this regard, there are many models that may suit a seller's needs. The six models provided below may be helpful.

1. **"Who? What? Why? How? How Much?"** In one form or another, many experts cite this simple approach. Every good value statement should answer these questions because they lie at the center of what a buyer is thinking. Rather than writing a value statement at the onset, the seller might list multiple responses to each question. For example, "who" asks the seller to identify a characteristic that defines the target

of the value proposition? "Who" may refer to an industry, market, geographic grouping, level in an organization, or executive who is faced with a particular challenge or opportunity. "What" describes the product, service, or solution. "Why" should convey the benefit the product provides to the buying organization. "How" describes how the seller's solution differs from the competition's. "How much" challenges the seller to quantify the change likely to result from the buyer's purchase. It's a simple template, but it moves the seller in the right direction.

2.  **The Job-to-Be-Done Model (JTBD).** Clay Christensen, Harvard University School of Business, shared a model that might provide insight into a customer's needs.[5] Christensen suggests that you ask yourself, "What is the 'job to be done' from the customer's perspective?" He writes, "'Job to be done' is shorthand for what an individual really seeks to accomplish in a given circumstance."[6] He recommends that the seller, innovator, or change agent think about what kind of experience a customer or buyer is attempting to create with their purchase. A homeowner isn't trying to own shelter at the cheapest price; they may be seeking a "work at home" environment that avoids long commutes. Focusing on their desired experience may be a better guideline to discover what a buyer truly needs than price or size. The point: sellers should explore underlying needs by asking, "What experience is my buyer trying to create?"

3.  **"The Combo."** The combo is a value statement that connects several benefits into a single sentence or two. For example, "Never has our industry seen a mobile device with this speed and range at this low a price." Or "If you are interested in a mobile solution that your customers can use with speed, convenience, and reliability, this is your best choice." Unfortunately, the temptation is to use "buzz" words that fail to convey the nature, impact, and scope of the benefit to the buying organization. The combo is often an attempt to flash several benefits in the hopes that one will connect with the buyer.

4. **Rackham's Model.** In their 1999 book *Rethinking the Salesforce,*[7] Neil Rackham and John DeVincentis argue that effective value propositions should include four elements: capability, impact, proof, and cost. Sellers would do well to make a master list of product capabilities, their impact on the buying organization, documentation of proof, and consideration of how best to position cost.

5. **Miller Heiman Group Model.** Robert Miller and Stephen Heiman, in their book *The New Conceptual Selling*[8], recommend a simple formula for identifying what they refer to as "Unique Strengths." First, the seller should list their strengths combining capabilities, benefits, and deliverables that would accrue to the buying organization from a purchase of the seller's product/solution. Second, eliminate any strength that is easily claimed by the competition. Third, the seller should ask, "So what?" "So what?" puts the seller in the buyer's "shoes." What benefit will the buyer gain from the purchase? The last test is "Prove it." What evidence can the seller offer that supports their claim?

6. **Williams-Saine Model.** Admittedly this is a simple model drawn from comments made by top producers across many industries. When we ask front-line sellers, "What do you include in messages that resonate best with buyers?" invariably, we hear some combination of the following five content elements:

   - **Customer's Problem:** statement of the problem or need from the buyer's perspective
   - **Impact If Unaddressed:** the problem's impact on the buying organization using the buyer's language
   - **Benefit of the Solution:** the benefit derived from the buying organization's purchase, including any quantification
   - **Our Proof of Claim:** documentation of value, including references to people, companies, and events
   - **Urgency to Act:** a reason for immediate change

## EXAMPLE: VALUE MESSAGE & TALKING POINTS

Let's try crafting a basic value message incorporating these five content elements. The first step is to treat each of the five content elements as a framework for organizing "talking points." Sellers should list powerful comments that might be included in their conversations, telephone calls, or discussions with a potential buyer.

Here's the selling situation. The seller offers enterprise solutions for cyber security, including equipment, software and consulting services. She is meeting with the number two person charged with cyber security for a $6B regional financial company. Let's look at the content elements and her talking points in the quotations below.

**Problem or Need:** "Virtually all companies are susceptible to security breaches. External players such as channel partners, suppliers, and consultants discover ninety-eight percent of all breaches. In other words, breaches are discovered by accident. In most companies, internal surveillance is woefully inadequate. Earlier this year, Forbes reported that cost of cybercrime is exceeding $400B annually."

**Impact:** "Security breaches can cost a company millions of dollars in lost business and legal expenses, not to mention the deterioration of a company's brand image in their market. Companies in financial services, healthcare, and ecommerce suffer the greatest losses."

**Benefits:** "For financial institutions, the first and foremost benefit lies in retaining customer confidence and loyalty. Our solution would allow the buyer to monitor, track, and address any system irregularities quickly with internal resources. It provides investors, company managers, and customers confidence that personal data as well as revenue is well protected."

**Proof:** "In 2013, Target's security breach (uncovered in the middle of holiday shopping) cost the company more than $215M in gross expenses. Research shows that, once discovered, the average breach is more than

201 days old. This means that the perpetrators breached the company's security, collected the customer data, and exited the system seven months prior to discovery."

**Urgency:** "Left undetected, cybercrime has an impact on companies that stretches well beyond current revenue streams. It can delay or stop new product releases, acquisitions, and other growth and expansion initiatives. Chief Information Officers and Chief Security Officers in Fortune 500 companies are treating cyber security with the highest level of priority. We would be happy to introduce you to your counterparts in other companies—some addressed the problem in time, while others found their delay to be very costly."

After building "talking points" the seller's next step is to compose hard hitting sentences that reflect problem, impact, benefit, proof and urgency—content that hit the mark with the Executive Buyer. Sellers may find that some content elements are more important to the buyer than others: choose appropriately.

> *"Cybercrime is a $400B hit to the bottom line of companies annually and analysts place mid-size regional institutions like yours at the top of the list of targets (problem).*
>
> *I have worked with companies, and can share case studies, (proof) where the impact was staggering—destroying revenue streams, damaging brand image and driving stock sell-offs by investor (impact).*
>
> *If we act promptly, we can customize a solution that neutralizes millions of dollars in financial risk (urgency). We can give your team the power to detect and defend against all types of cyber breeches. We will train your staff and help you build analytic models that predict where breeches are most likely to occur and how best to insulate your operations (benefit). It's time to be a hero…not a victim."*

At this point, the seller has a thirty-second message in addition to several talking points around the five content elements. The third step is to get feedback. Test the message with other sellers, coaches, and colleagues. Then shorten the message one last time.

At this juncture, we have a value message targeted to an executive and surrounded by talking points that can be delivered in person, via an email, or left as a voice message. Remember you can deliver all or part of your value message as appropriate to the conversation.

### Bake Your Value Messages into Your Proposal

Your proposal is a critical culmination of all your value messaging, and it must be compelling and clear enough to sell itself, as it circulates throughout your prospect's business. You will not always have the opportunity to explain your proposal, so it's extremely important that your value messages are represented effectively in your proposal.

## FIVE TEMPTATIONS TO AVOID

1. **One-size-fits-all customer value messages.** No matter how powerful the message may seem, different customers at different levels of the buyer organization have different needs and priorities. Don't dilute the impact of value messages with great selling points that don't matter.

2. **Values that don't differentiate or resonate.** Strike benefits that can be easily claimed by the competition. Their "me too" approach will commoditize your products as well as theirs.

3. **Mistaking a product feature as a value.** Focus on what the product does for the customer. They want outcomes. The adage fits: "They are buying holes, not drills."

4. **Mistaking buyer curiosity for urgency.** Urgency has its own language. Use it to create a more compelling statement.

5. **Overlooking hidden sources of risk.** All purchases represent a risk. Minimize or control risk for buyers who are risk averse.

**Key Points to Remember for Buyer-Centered Sellers**

1.  Sellers must craft compelling value statements that differentiate their product or solution from competitive options, convey a benefit that connects with a specific buyer's needs, and provide documentation that supports the seller's claim.

2.  For every value message, a buyer will evaluate your value claims, differentiation, proof, their risk, and urgency.

3.  There are at least six models that are used to develop value messages. Sellers should pick one that works for them and their organization.

4.  Many sellers, irrespective of their product, service, or solution, position themselves as consultants who assist their customers in solving a problem or capitalizing on an opportunity. Consultants face a different challenge in crafting a value proposition. Why? Because the seller or consultant is the product.

5.  In sales, it's expertise, experience, and market insight that matter. This is why it is so important to develop a compelling value proposition. A sales professional's experience with enterprise-wide solutions, global implementations, or migration to new service platforms can serve as a strong value framework that draws attention and interest from your customer and partners.

6.  The Williams-Saine value messaging platform consists of the following components: the customer's problem, impact if left unaddressed, benefit of your solution or claim, proof of claim and urgency to act.

7.  Always perform a final review of your proposal to ensure that you've adequately amplified your value messages throughout the document and in a way that allows the proposal to sell for you in your absence.

## THE SKILL CHALLENGE

In order to become more effective and buyer centered, what skill can you identify from the content in this chapter that requires skill and practice? Please write it here or on a separate sheet of paper.

_____

_____

_____

_____

_____

_____

_____

_____

_____

_____

_____

_____

_____

_____

_____

_____

_____

_____

# Chapter 6

# Jewels from the Junkyard: Resuscitating Stalled Opportunities

"Stalled deals plague the sales profession, clogging pipelines, ruining forecasts, and causing untold frustration."

Jeb Blount—Author of *Sales EQ*

Many sales professionals have a sales funnel that looks a bit like a salvage yard. It's filled with sales opportunities they don't pursue and potential clients that won't call back. They represent selling processes that were started and abandoned, and buying processes that seemed to evaporate overnight. At plan reviews, there are ample excuses, stories, and fabrications to go around.

The number of stalled and abandoned opportunities is staggering. CSO Insights reported that the average win rate of deals that sellers forecast to win in 2017 was a meager 41.3%[1]. Think about what this means. Either sellers are grossly inaccurate in assessing their competitive position, sellers are overly optimistic in qualifying an opportunity, or many opportunities are simply not awarded. Our guess is that all three possibilities play a role.

Over the years, we've reviewed thousands of sales funnels, and the more we probe, the more we are convinced that many of these abandoned, neglected, and stalled opportunities could be salvaged. In fact, these stalled opportunities offer the tenacious buyer-centered seller a rich list of potential sales.

### Story: Chasing a "Stretch" Sales Goal

Several years ago, we were helping a sales executive build a road map for achieving a "stretch" sales goal thrown to him by the C-suite. As we were conducting a region-by-region review, he continued to fall short of goal. It took a few hours for us to realize that the team members were ignoring stalled opportunities from the prior year. Team members reasoned if they couldn't close a deal in the previous year, they were wasting their time pursuing it in the current year.

That is wrong, dead wrong, and absolutely wrong! We calculated the potential revenue of stalled opportunities from the prior year and were amazed. We eliminated opportunities currently serviced by successful and entrenched competitors. Stalled opportunities from the prior year represented a 19% increase in potential funnel revenue.

The sales executive got his territory sellers on a conference call and shared a plan to contact, requalify, and pursue target opportunities. We built a program of best practices. Everyone agreed to apply a score-card to determine whether an opportunity was "probable, possible, or unlikely." There wasn't a lot of time to nurture these opportunities so we agreed to start at the top: go find the Executive Buyer or use a credible relationship to lever access to the Executive Buyer and bring a powerful story. Marketing contributed with a mini-playbook focused on stalled opportunities. Everyone agreed to a thirty-day trial period for each opportunity. If the initial contact with the Executive Buyer didn't yield measureable results within a month, then we moved the opportunity out of the sales funnel and focused on other selling activity.

The end of the story is wild and wonderful. Did the team make their stretch goal? It was coming down to the close of the fiscal year, and the team was running short of goal, but sales and finance had pulled every financial and accounting trick they could legally employ to boost revenue. They were a little more than $10,000 short of goal, and the hourglass was running out of sand. But the Sales Executive felt he owed it to his team to get them across the finish line. He targeted several opportunities where he knew the Executive Buyer. He spent a week traversing the U.S. and returned with $213,000 of additional revenue. He realized three lessons: "Stretch" goals aren't impossible. Old contacts can be valuable contacts. Stalled opportunities may be jewels.

---

### The Challenge of Buyer-Centered Selling

**The Buyer's Dilemma: Often faced with supporting multiple complex initiatives, buyers are torn by conflicting buying processes. One process is aborted so that a higher priority project can be completed. Internal politics, production changes, and funding issues are a few of the factors that can force buying processes to be delayed or stalled.** What may seem to be an orderly process to the outside supplier can actually be chaotic.

**The Seller's Challenge: Most sellers are faced with several sales opportunities that stall or derail. The challenge lies in knowing how to re-qualify the opportunity, investigate whether the "buying context" has changed, and determine what actions would make buyers more receptive to the seller's product or solution.** Too often when an opportunity stalls, it leads to a series of bad decisions by the seller. Instead of working to discover the cause of the delay and creating a renewed sense of urgency, sellers often disconnect and assume the buying process will resume where it left off when they decide to revisit the opportunity.

---

In this chapter, we'll explore what constitutes a stalled opportunity, why deals stall, and how sellers can help buyers revitalize and re-energize a stalled process.

## STALLED OR DORMANT—DEAD OR ABANDONED?

Let's begin by differentiating a stalled opportunity from a dormant one. Quite simply, a stalled opportunity describes a buying process that has stopped, derailed, or become obstructed. Sellers and managers often refer to an opportunity that has been "moved to the back burner," implying that what was boiling is now lukewarm or cold. There is no discernible progress or detectable action by the buyer or buying team. Some are deferred temporarily; others have come to a complete halt. As an experienced seller, you know that, when left unattended, time kills all deals.[2]

> "A stalled opportunity describes a buying process that has stopped, derailed, or become obstructed."

Often our initial awareness of an opportunity that has stalled is the termination of some scheduled buying activity. The buying team cancelled a bid meeting or delayed (without rescheduling) a planned meeting. Time passes without contact or explanation. Then the excuses start to pile up. "We were getting too close to the holidays." "We've been asked to 'clear the decks' for a new product release."

Whatever... When we review sales funnels, we always investigate the "time dating" on stalled opportunities. When did the opportunity first surface? When was the last documentable action by the buying team? What explanation did they provide? What modified timeline did they share? It is not unusual to find stalled opportunities that are a year or eighteen months old. Often sellers assume "when the buyer is ready, he/she will give us a call." Well... if that was the case, all we would need is a call center.

> Dormant opportunities refer to leads where the seller and prospective buyer have stopped communicating or never communicated.

Dormant describes an opportunity without any activity or communication. Dormant leads are ones with whom the seller has never communicated or stopped communicating. Some sales teams have formal protocols for purging or reassigning dormant leads. Many companies continue to include dormant prospects in their funnels and databases.

To summarize, leads are classified as dormant because the selling and buying organizations have never communicated or stopped communicating, resulting in zero business activity. Stalled sales opportunities reflect a buying process that has become delayed, derailed, or dismantled. More often than not, once a sales opportunity stalls, the seller becomes frustrated, and communication stops.

## Why Are Stalled Opportunities Worth Pursuing?

Stalled opportunities can provide a nice (and often unexpected) bump in revenue achievement. Let's take a hypothetical example. Suppose "Sarah" is midway through the sales year and has achieved only 38% of her quota. The last half of the year looks a little better after she considers her active opportunities and adds up the known and likely sales. However, Sarah is afraid the year-end number is still going to fall a bit short at 90% of quota.

Is it realistic to re-engage a buyer for an opportunity that seems to have "gone dark" in Q1 of this year or another opportunity that stalled in Q4 of last year? The question facing Sarah isn't, "How can I work harder to sell more?" The question is, "How can I enrich my sales funnel with two or three opportunities that can be converted within a short time frame?"

Let's consider some reasons why stalled opportunities may provide excellent additions to a seller's funnel.

- The seller may have mapped the buying process and may have solid information about stakeholders and buying team members. This information may prove valuable for jump-starting the opportunity.
- The seller may have developed a formative relationship with the Executive Buyer and buying team members. This gives the seller the ability to act quickly and effectively to re-qualify the opportunity.

- Frustrated competitors may have lost interest. When a buying process gets pushed to the back burner, it's frustrating for all suppliers except the incumbent. The competitive landscape may have thinned out.
- The buying team may have resolved obstacles such as funding, competing priorities, and leadership challenges.
- The problem or challenge faced by the buying organization may have grown out of control, creating a heightened sense of urgency.

It could be well worth the time and energy to re-connect, qualify, and pursue or discard these opportunities. Last year's trash may be this year's treasure.

## EIGHT REASONS WHY SALES OPPORTUNITIES STALL

Opportunities stall for a variety of reasons. Let's consider the eight most common causes.

| Buy-Sell Disconnect | No Road Map for Change | Unclear Financial Return | No Differentiation Among Solutions |
| Failure to Reach Consensus | Competing Priorities | Covert Influencers | Risk Aversion |

Figure 6-1: Why Sales Opportunities Stall

**Buy-Sell Disconnect.** In this scenario, the seller has failed to connect the selling process to the buyer's process. Sometimes sellers get ahead of the buying process. Buyer-centered sellers have a clear view of where the buyer is in the decision-making process and help them think through each stage (or job or task). Are they still focused on recognizing the problem? Are they looking at options and comparing solutions? Or, are they comparing best-choice solutions with the status quo? It's difficult for sellers to connect their product, service, or solution to specific business problems if they can't gauge where the buyer is, where he/she is going, and what obstacles need to be overcome. The reality is that different stakeholders can be at different phases.

**No Road Map for Change.** The executive team may have a clear understanding of the size, scope, and urgency of the problem. What they don't have is a "road map" of action steps and timelines that would lead them toward the selection and implementation of an appropriate solution. Sellers cannot move the sale forward unless the buying team has a clear road map for change. They need someone who knows the path and can help them anticipate obstacles and manage change. One way to prevent stalled opportunities is to co-build the road map with the buying team as appropriate and as early as possible in the buying cycle. Buyer-centered sellers help customers outline and simplify a pathway for change while anticipating obstacles and challenges.

**Unclear Financial Return.** Few executive teams are willing to invest resources in solving a problem without a documentable financial return. If the problem they are facing has too many "unknowns," the initiative goes to the back burner until someone can quantify the size and timing of the return. It is the seller's responsibility to clearly define the cost of inaction. Put simply, this is the measurable difference between the current state and the future, desired state when using your product, service, or solution. It's important to recognize that a financial return can take many different forms to different buyers. One may be looking for increased revenue, while another is looking for speed and efficiency or reduced cost.

**No Differentiation Among Solutions.** It is unclear how well any solution will perform or resolve the problem at hand. Consequently, there is no compelling reason to act. Sometimes a buying team is faced with one or more potential solutions, but no one on the team has the experience to identify the best solution. Buyer-centered sellers help stakeholders understand the relevance and unique benefit of their product or solution. If you haven't created a compelling value difference among solutions, don't expect stakeholders to translate a garbled message into a cause for action.

**Failure to Reach Consensus.** Many Executive Buyers are looking for more than a plurality of votes—they want a stakeholder consensus. They want a decision that everyone can support. Buyers want to avoid a situation where a vocal minority continues to "second guess" the majority decision. So when a leading supplier fails to achieve a consensus, many buying processes stall or derail.

**Competing Priorities.** Other projects may have surfaced that require financial and operational resources. Pressure to change can arise quickly as market conditions fluctuate. Changes in the competitive landscape, financial downturns, or difficulty with a product release can change corporate priorities quickly. Often the budgetary allocations, especially for new and previously unbudgeted projects, will shift as priorities change, taking away financial support.

**Covert Influencers.** We all recognize the need to connect with each influential stakeholder. But it's easier said than done. Some influencers take a more "covert" role. For example, a stakeholder may resist taking on a committee role but will continue to influence voting members "behind the scenes." Other influencers may be reluctant to change. They sow seeds of doubt and fear that undermine the committee's efforts to build a working majority.

**Risk Aversion.** We know what you're thinking: we held the heavy ballistics until last. That's correct! Risk is the stop-dead-in-your-tracks buying process killer. Stakeholders are likely to be very cautious, especially on big ticket items. One or more stakeholders may see a "loss" in supporting your solution. This may be perceived or real. In any event, it paralyzes the stakeholder from acting on your behalf. The safer solution for now means to "stay the course" and defer the decision process.

## HOW BUYER-CENTERED SELLERS REVITALIZE STALLED BUYING PROCESSES

While the plan for revitalizing a stalled opportunity depends on the situational and contextual variables that drove the opportunity to the back burner, there are five approaches that buyer-centered sellers find helpful.

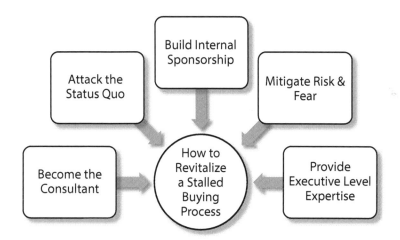

Figure 6-2: How Buyer-Centered Sellers Revitalize a Stalled Buying Process

**1. Become the Consultant.** Sometimes our desire to sell impairs our ability to provide valued assistance to an organization. Try to determine why the initiative has shifted to the back burner—then offer consulting assistance. Do they need someone to break down the problem into manageable components? Do they need to calculate and document ROI? Would they benefit from a case study that would help outline clearly a course of action? Would a customer's testimonial elevate interest?

**Recommended Action:** The seller should focus on understanding what the buyers know, want to know, and need to know. Develop a communication plan—along with meetings and interviews—to provide insight and elevate their understanding. Focus on helping them better understand their problem or need, gain a better grasp of solutions and options, and appreciate the seller's resources and capabilities. Don't hesitate to simplify the process or compress timelines by delegating responsibilities. This may be exactly what the Executive Buyer wants.

**2. Attack the Status Quo.** When a sales opportunity stalls, it's easy to conclude that no decision has been rendered and that the opportunity may resurface on its own in the near future. Let's suggest an alternative reality for you as a seller: you competed against the status quo and lost! Sellers often assume wrongly that there are no active competitors and that it is their sole opportunity to eventually win. The seller's real competition is to "do nothing" and maintain the status quo. Buyer-centered sellers are quick to take a fresh look at the competition and develop a strategy to undermine support for the status quo. They build a business case to show the "cost of doing nothing."

**Recommended Action:** The seller should identify the status quo as the presumptive favorite, develop powerful messages that will resonate with buyers and executives, and focus on differentiating the product or solution from the existing option while mitigating risk. Consider building and circulating a business case that supports claims.

**3. Build Internal Sponsorship.** Often there are one or two executives who stand to lose the most if the problem is left unaddressed. Internal users need to grasp the benefit of providing leadership for the initiative. Politics can sink many seaworthy boats.

**Recommended Action:** Buyer-centered sellers identify and cultivate an executive or group of supporters who can provide internal sponsorship for the initiative. Arm them with essential information, and use their connections to gain traction for your product or service. Users can be a powerful force in swaying a decision. Mobilize users to request your solution.

**4. Mitigate Fear & Risk.** Often buying teams are plagued by discussions that raise concerns about the product or solution. "How sure are we that any product will perform as advertised?" "What if we encounter an emergency? How will they respond?" "Are there additional or hidden costs for maintenance or training?" The seller's responsibility is to assuage fear and "buyer anxiety." Help buyers have confidence in your product and implementation plan. Fear of an impending loss or unanticipated threat can quickly fuel a buyer's resistance to change. Advocates for the status quo are quick to portray change as fraught with unnecessary risk. The seller's challenge is to shift buyers' focus and show that the true risk and threat of failure would be to maintain the status quo.

**Recommended Action:** Buyer-centered sellers develop a communication plan that addresses buyer anxieties and promotes confidence in the seller, the product, and the selling organization. Consider providing testimonials, client references, case studies, and research results from product trials. For a deeper dive into how risk can undermine a seller's opportunity, consider Chapter 7, "Scared Straight: Selling to the Risk Averse Buyer." You may be surprised at the power that risk carries in swaying stakeholders.

**5. Provide Executive Level Expertise.** Sponsor an executive briefing for all stakeholders. Many companies, especially in the technology sector, sponsor executive briefings to help educate potential customers. Let's be clear. An executive briefing is not a sales pitch—it's a forum wherein experts and specialists share their insight surrounding a defined problem. The topic, agenda, and content are designed with the customer's interests in mind. The intent is to bring the potential customer "up to speed." An executive briefing has three benefits for the selling organization.

- It positions the seller and the selling team as consultants—not sales representatives.
- It conveys a sense of urgency that can bring a project to the front burner.
- It connects the buying and selling organizations at a more senior level.

**Recommended Action:** The seller should consider a means of "showcasing" expertise while educating the customer. Develop an agenda around the customer's concerns and needs with zero pressure to sell and 100% focus on what the prospective buyers want to know, discuss, or clarify.

### Develop a Stalled Opportunity Campaign

When confronted with a stalled opportunity, the seller has a choice. They can ignore the opportunity and pray that the buying team will experience an epiphany that drives them to re-engage, or they can become a part of the solution by driving the re-engagement process.

Buyer-centered sellers re-qualify their options. They select one or two targets and develop a campaign to mobilize the stalled buying processes. Sellers who choose this course of action should consider the following questions in developing their strategy to energize a stalled opportunity:

- **What financial, operational, or administrative events may have deflated the organization's commitment to change?** As important as the seller thinks his/her initiative is to the buying organization, the customer's business is dynamic, and his/her priorities can change quickly. It is important during every sales call to ask, "Has anything changed since our last conversation?" And, "Is this project still a priority for everyone?"

- **Have you mapped the buy-sell process, including measurable actions required to move the buying process from stage to stage?** It is common for sellers to find themselves charging forward while the buying team is still trying to fully understand the nature and scope of their needs. It's easy for the buying and selling processes to become misaligned. Ask, "Where am I in the selling process?" "Where is the buyer in the buying process?"

- **Have you correctly identified the Executive Buyer and secured his/her buy-in to your solution?** Does the Executive Buyer require a business case? How does your solution link to a key performance indicator on his/her dashboard? Will the

Executive Buyer make the decision or will they rely on majority rule or a consensus? If you know the terminology of his/her KPIs, link your solution to that using the same "language."

- **Have you identified compelling strengths that differentiate your solution?** Often prospects become paralyzed when comparing several products with similar capabilities. Help them choose by focusing your messages on strengths that matter to the prospect and differentiate your product or service. There are three keys to differentiation. First, your solution must be relevant to vital initiatives of the buying organization. Second, your capabilities must be unique or better than the competition. Third, it must create urgency. Be sure to focus on strengths that impact measurable results in the buyer's organization. They must answer the question "So, why is this important and now?" for your customer.

- **Are you asking the right questions to uncover the size and scope of the buyer's needs?** How comprehensive was the "discovery" process? Who should be interviewed again? Have allegiances changed or shifted? What steps has the buyer taken to get educated and informed? Have you identified how different functions in the buying organization are impacted by the issue and how each will benefit from a solution?

- **Are you adapting your value message to resonate with each stakeholder?** Are you using their language to capture their perceptions? What key performance indicators matter to each stakeholder? Do any of the stakeholders view a change as a risk to their position, reputation, or job security?

- **Have you conveyed a sense of urgency?** Does the buying team understand the cost of a lost opportunity? Have you presented a strong case for risk-free implementation of your solution?

■ **Have you calculated and shared the cost of "doing nothing"?** Often it is easy for buyers to overlook the full breadth of costs incurred by internal legacy solutions. The cost of doing nothing is not exclusively a financial challenge. Consider whose interests are not being served.

### Calculate the Cost of Inaction (COI)

The Cost of Inaction (COI) is the business and opportunity costs associated with the organization's failure to adopt a new solution. While the formula for estimating the cost of doing nothing is different by industry and company, finance and procurement executives often overlook the "cost" from their failure to act. Buyer-centered sellers invest effort into calculating known costs and identifying other expenses or opportunity benefits that are being ignored:

1. Loss of revenue opportunity (the compromise of a potential revenue stream)
2. Reduced speed to market, especially with customer-enabled solutions
3. Costly customer dissatisfaction and potential defection
4. Market share lost to competitors
5. Failure to capture future cost reductions that are not immediate, such as downsizing or the elimination of training expenses
6. Cost of repairs, maintenance, expansion of present solution
7. Price inflation of products in subsequent years
8. Outdated warrantees and maintenance agreements
9. Loss of talent and human resources
10. Delivery problems and out-of-stock issues with outdated products
11. Lagging on the technology curve—a future cost associated with not keeping up with changing technology
12. Failure to achieve better outcomes, e.g., technical, clinical, financial, operational, etc.

### Reflections for the Sales Manager

While the sales representative is mulling whether to spend his/her time on a stalled sales initiative, the sales manager or executive should be mulling over what to do with the account listed in the sales funnel. Is the opportunity still viable? Should it remain in the sales funnel or be removed? Is there some disconnect between the customer and the sales representative? Should the account be transferred to another member of the sales team? Does the team have a solid strategy in place?

When a sales manager is faced with two or three stalled opportunities in a single sales funnel, the problems begin to multiply. If you, as a sales manager, do nothing, it can lower your close ratio, lengthen the projected sales cycle, and introduce additional sources of error in your revenue projections. Does the team have a disciplined approach to "losing fast," i.e., making an early determination that the opportunity is not viable and getting it out of the funnel before too much effort is expended on an opportunity that is not qualified or winnable?

This becomes a great coaching opportunity. As a sales manager, you have the opportunity to help your sales professional review the situation and develop a buyer-centered action plan.

### Key Points to Remember for Buyer-Centered Sellers

1. The seller's initial responsibility is to "re-qualify" the opportunity. The seller should apply a scorecard to the opportunity and determine whether it is a good sales opportunity, a good fit for the seller at this time, and a good prospect as a customer.

2. Uncover the "why." Why did the buying initiative stall? What in the "buying context" may have derailed the buying process? Was it a competitor? Financial considerations? Competing priorities? If you don't know the "why," it's difficult to plan an effective campaign.

3. Discover the "who." Buying initiatives seldom die by accident. Someone moved the opportunity aside. The seller's challenge is to identify who disconnected life support systems and who has the authority and influence to reclassify the initiative as a high priority.

4. Stalled opportunities may be an excellent addition to your sales funnel if you have already mapped the buying process and established a relationship with a key executive or user.

5. Opportunities may stall for a variety of reasons: a disconnect between the buying and selling processes, unclear ROI, the lack of an internal sponsor, or risks that paralyze decision making.

6. When crafting a plan to re-energize a stalled opportunity, consider adding the following to your game plan: Become more consultative (help the stakeholder understand their underlying needs), attack the status quo (uncover the "cost of inactivity"), and expand your internal base of sponsors.

## THE SKILL CHALLENGE

In order to become more effective and buyer centered, what skill can you identify from the content in this chapter that requires skill and practice? Please write it here or on a separate sheet of paper.

---

---

---

---

---

---

---

---

# Chapter 7

# Scared Straight: Selling to the Risk Averse Buyer

"Allowing your prospective client to run off to assess the risks, resolve their concerns, and address their own fears is a poor strategy."

Anthony Iannarino—Author of *The Lost Art of Closing*

We have all been burned by events we couldn't predict, outcomes we couldn't prevent, or consequences we couldn't control. Some of us view these circumstances with complete optimism and confidence, while others view the same circumstances with feelings of dread and fear. It's part of the amazing calculus of logic and emotion that makes us different.

How we perceive risk in any given circumstance is due to a unique combination of cognitive factors such as test data, performance records, research reports, internet articles, price, and delivery records. Our risk perception is also affected by emotional factors such as prior experiences, trigger events, and stories and events shared by others.

Every day, buyers are faced with two options: keep doing what they are doing or change. Every decision to change carries an element of risk as well as the attendant emotional baggage that we call "fear," "worry," or "concern." Despite a seller's best efforts to convince a buyer that a purchase is completely without risk, some buyers are overcome by fears that can slow or derail a buying decision. Just because the risk-reward calculation works, it doesn't always ensure that a last-minute second wave of fear won't overwhelm the buyer and stall the deal or convince the buyer that the status quo is the safest course of action.

## Story: Clinical Metrics

A few months ago, a sales professional and the CEO of a small start-up software company made a call on a department head at a local hospital. The product they were selling helps a hospital department collect specific clinical metrics to improve patient outcomes. There are a host of benefits from this product such as analytics on equipment utilization and manpower deployment. When the department director saw the demo of the product, she loved it. In fact, she was so excited about it that she took us to meet John—an important team lead in her department. John would be the primary user of the software.

After our colleague demonstrated the product, John leaned back in his chair, crossed his legs, and then asked, "Why did you design the interface that way? Why can't I get a report from this screen? I need X on this screen, and it's not there."

The President of the software company was a bit overwhelmed, so he asked for a five-minute break. During the interlude, he said to his seller, "I thought this deal was won, but now it looks like we are going to lose it because of John. Do you have any ideas?"

When the CEO and seller went back into the buyer's office, the sales representative said, "John, let's forget about the product for a moment. Instead, tell us about your job." Then John said the following: "I do what that software does." In effect, John was telling them that if his institution purchased that software, he would be out of a job. The benefits of the product meant nothing to John when compared to his perception that he might lose his job.

As soon as the CEO and seller recognized the risk, they mitigated John's fear, by showing him how the software would enhance his job and expand his value to the organization. Nice sale!

---

## The Challenge of Buyer-Centered Selling

*The Buyer's Dilemma:* **Every purchase involves some element of risk. Stakeholders are challenged to balance the business outcomes (impact of your solution minus the cost) of a purchase decision with the downside risks—both personal and business—as perceived at the moment.** In many cases, the preferred supplier isn't the one offering the least expensive product but the company that can best predict, minimize, and correct sources of risk. Buyers are struggling to craft a plan that insulates themselves and their organization from harm.

*The Seller's Challenge:* **Buyer-Centered Sellers Help Buyers Manage the Perceptions of Risk and Feelings of Fear That Can Undermine Their Willingness to Change.** The seller's ability to help buyers put aside fears can make the difference between winning and losing a deal. Why? Purchasing decisions often involve several or many stakeholders, each harboring different perceptions of risk and fears of failure.

---

Buyer-centered sellers assist stakeholders in crafting a plan that minimizes risk and fear. Without a plan and the commitment of appropriate resources, risk can paralyze a buyer and stall a buying process.

During this chapter, we'll explore the relationship between risk aversion and fear of failure, ways to mitigate perceptions of risk, the various types of risk that can plague a buying decision, and how to uncover a buyer's perceptions of risk.

## WHAT IS RISK AVERSION?

> Risk aversion is a disposition to act or avoid action based upon a person's perception of risk.

Risk is the chance that something can go wrong. Risk aversion is a disposition to act or avoid action based upon a person's perception of risk. It can characterize a buyer's disposition at any point in the buying process. But risk aversion has become an organizational condition that underlies the structure and decision processes of individuals. It's the reason today's sellers are facing committees instead of department heads, why sales cycles are taking months instead of weeks. It's the reason buying groups are insisting on a consensus instead of a plurality of votes to make a purchasing decision.

In a 2017 Demand Gen Report, researchers shared three results that help explain the impact of risk avoidance on an organization. First, 59% of surveyed buyers reported they had installed formal buying groups or committees to oversee the purchasing process and ensure the integrity of the purchase.[1]

Organizations have concluded they can best insulate themselves from purchasing risks by seeking as much input as possible while ensuring that any forward-moving change has undergone responsible scrutiny. Their fallback position is the status quo or current state.

A second finding from the survey was that 52% of the buyers reported the size of buying committees had increased significantly in the last year.[2] This is bad news for sellers who are attempting to break the hold of an entrenched supplier.

Third, 86% of buyers reported that the timing of purchasing decisions can be increased or slowed, based upon the needs of the relevant business units and other organizational priorities.[3] The impact on sellers is clear cut: complex B2B opportunities are harder to sell, the time requirements are greater, the discovery process is more complex, and many of these new stakeholders are experienced negotiators and process managers who hold an expertise in supplier management.

While risk assessment is, in large measure, a rational or cognitive function of the large portion of the brain, fear of failure is an emotional product of the small brain.

Fear of failure and risk avoidance can do much more than complicate the selling process. It can stifle the creativity and innovation of an organization by discouraging change. Risk avoidance can derail entrepreneurship and undermine improvements essential to growth.[4]

## HOW BUYER-CENTERED SELLERS MITIGATE BUYER RISK AND FEAR

Risk and fear are a powerhouse duo that can drive or paralyze decision-making. Corporate Visions reported that executives are far more likely to make risky decisions when they want to avoid a loss (loss-aversion) than when they are driven by acquiring or gaining something they don't presently have. The implication for sales professionals is clear. When crafting value messages, sellers are more likely to have a greater impact on buyers if they craft value messages and frame their solution as ones that minimize risk of loss. When sellers are attempting to renew a contract and retain services, they should emphasize the risk associated with change.

Consider the following ways buyer-centered sellers minimize a buyer's perception of risk and fear of change.

1. **Plan Frequent and Open Communication.** The best method of addressing risk and fear is through frequent and open communication between buyer and seller. While face-to-face meetings are helpful or even therapeutic, don't underestimate the value of emails and phone calls to address sudden issues or share important successes. *Every complex sales proposal would do well to include a communication plan for all layers of the buying organization—users, technical advisors, process managers, and executive level buyers.*

2. **Identify Review Processes.** Buyer-centered sellers often include in their proposal an audit or review process that contains benchmarks, performance thresholds, timelines, and potential resets. Executive Buyers don't want to know that "things are going well." They want to know: "Are we precisely where we want to be at this point in time? If not, why not? How will we get there?" *A best practice is to establish a plan with "go/no-go" steps and action requirements for the buyer and seller.*

3. **Plan On-Site Technical Expertise.** *At times, an on-site technical specialist or project manager is just what the buying team needs.* A "voice on the phone" just won't address a buyer's concerns, but everyone sleeps easier when there's a competent technical specialist on site.

4. **Solicit Frontline & User Feedback.** Even prior to the award of a contract or issuance of a purchase order, it may be helpful to consult with frontline users to gauge their concerns and ask for their support. A buyer-centered seller can quickly build credibility by explaining, "I've just spoken with several of the frontline users, and here's what they told me." *It's all about the seamless integration of a selling team and a buying organization.*

5. **Share Relevant Testimonials, References & Case Studies.** Stories, events, case studies, and professional references combine emotional and cognitive factors that can minimize the perception of risk and mitigate the emotional factors that elevate fear and anxiety. *Buyer-centered sellers are proactive in offering valued resources.*

6. **Customize Planning Documents with Realistic Timelines.** *A best practice in change management is to customize plans and timelines to address the interests and desires of the buying organization.* "One size fits all" planning creates significant implementation obstacles that can undermine a seller's proposal. Buyers want road maps that embrace their critical decision points and timelines.

7. **Build "Change Coalitions."** Buyer-centered sellers identify concentrations of supporters or early adopters. These are individuals that want your solution, have influence within their organization, and will build consensus for your solution. *Buyer-centered sellers often rely on "change coalitions" to reach out to others and expand the network of supporters, advocates, and champions.* When a solution requires a complex implementation process, consider building support groups.

8. **Engage Pockets of Resistance.** Every buying organization has pockets of workers who are resistant to change. Many buying executives harbor concerns that these pockets may undermine or delay the implementation of change. *Buyer-centered sellers have a plan that identifies, engages, and cultivates support among the forces of resistance.*

9. **Identify "Owners" and "Loaners."** In every buying organization, there may be stakeholders who are not included in the evaluation and review process. But that doesn't mean they don't communicate with members of the buying team. In fact, "owners" (those who have some ownership of business processes that are impacted by the buying decision) can raise significant anxiety and fear with a couple of well-placed phone calls. *During the selling process, buyer-centered sellers try to uncover "owners" who need to be contacted by the seller or selling team.*

"Loaners" are those members of the buying organization who are not directly involved with business activities impacted by the buying decision but have occasional contact. It may be the case that the "loaner" shares a database with daily users ("owners"). "Loaners" may provide internal services to the "owner," like training, marketing, or financial services.

### Story: "We Can't Allow That to Happen to Us."

Carson, a sales manager for an international architectural firm, was on the verge of a huge sale that would make his annual quota and his bosses' number as well. He had worked hard to win a $6M contract to develop architectural plans to renovate the city-owned arena into a multi-purpose facility that would handle conventions, exhibits, sports tournaments, and even rodeos.

Carson knew that the selection committee was talking exclusively to him. His days were filled with meetings with city departments to better understand their requirements for the facility and evening briefings and presentations with the City Council. The ability to lure additional services to the city arena stirred visions of new revenue streams for the committee.

Over the weekend, Carson got a call from the mayor, Caroline Mays. It was not good news! The mayor explained that a similar project in the next state—one that the City Council was using as a model to cultivate public support and assuage voter fears—had been halted because of critical planning flaws. While Carson's firm had no involvement with the project, fear of failure can be a powerful deal killer. Caroline seemed determined to slow or halt the project. "We can't allow that to happen to us. It would be a disaster!"

The mayor shared her knowledge of the issues that warranted a work stoppage. She was concerned that vocal public objections would grow and ultimately kill the project. In city government, there are financial, political, and personal fears that can quickly complicate or kill buying decisions. Carson asked for the opportunity to investigate the situation and provide an appraisal of the project.

A week later, Carson called the mayor and set up a Council briefing. In preparation for the session, Carson:

- Identified all the shortcoming problems that threatened the "sister" project
- Explored other issues that might arise and create delays (such as weather, product availability)
- Made a list of financial challenges and how the Council could predict budgetary over-runs
- Formulated timelines and benchmarks for different phases of the overall project

- Calculated revenue lost from a twelve-month, an eighteen-month, and a twenty-four month delay

A day later Caroline called and shared the following. "The Council was greatly impressed by your investigative work and problem solving skills. One conclusion we reached was that we needed to proceed with the planning at the architectural level and that you are an essential player in our plans. The Council has authorized me to contract with your firm, and we look forward to working with you."

## Prepare Responses to a Buyer's Questions About Risk

Buying decisions are not always based on which selling company provides the best solution (especially in complex B2B sales) but on which company has the best ability to assess risks and develop a risk-free implementation plan. Sophisticated buyers expect sellers to anticipate the process of implementation. Who will take responsibility? What resources will be required? Who will take ownership when something goes wrong?

During the sales process, stakeholders and Executive Buyers attempt to gauge the degree of disruption created by their buying decision and how prepared the selling team is to prevent the disruption or respond to it, if necessary. When selling complex or enterprise-wide solutions, sellers must address many critical concerns. Below are key questions that require compelling answers from the selling team. If sellers fail to provide convincing answers to these buyers' questions, they may inadvertently elevate a buyer's perceptions of risk and fear.

- Who from the selling organization "owns" the responsibility for preventing or responding to disruption?
- Who is responsible for keeping the buying organization informed during all stages of transition or implementation?
- How frequently can we expect updates, and what content can we anticipate?

- In what ways will you solicit feedback from our team and customize the implementation to meet our needs and concerns?
- Who from the selling organization will serve as an "executive liaison" to our organization?
- Who from your client list would be available to share their experiences with us?
- What plans have you designed to overcome resistance to change in our organization?
- What plans have you made to ensure speedy and effective response to a system's failure?
- What assurances do we have that your implementation plan won't result in disruption to our business processes?
- If there is a disruption, who would take responsibility?
- How will we know that the implementation is complete and functioning as promised?
- In the event of an accident or malfunction of equipment, who would assume liability?

While the responses to these questions hit at the heart of customer service, a deal may never reach fruition unless the seller or selling team can ensure the buyer that plans exist to predict, prevent, and repair the sources of risk.

## Uncovering Buyer Perceptions of Risk

A buyer's risk has two components: the probability that something will go wrong and the negative consequences if it does.

Every buying decision involves some level of risk. Because people make buying decisions, everyone involved in a purchase decision must carefully weigh their personal and professional risks when making a recommendation for a specific solution and for a provider. It's human nature to mitigate risk. No one wants to be part of a poor buying decision, and no one wants to be a casualty because of it.

Buyer-centered sellers encourage "risk discussions" to remove the anxiety from each stakeholder's mind and to move the deal forward instead of allowing it to stall. Be careful to address all questions of risk.

## MITIGATING TWELVE TYPES OF BUYER RISK

There are twelve different types of buyer risk that sellers may encounter.

| Types of Buyer Risk | |
|---|---|
| 1. Financial | 7. Physical |
| 2. Unfamiliarity | 8. Time |
| 3. Personal | 9. Natural |
| 4. Operational | 10. Execution |
| 5. Resource Allocation | 11. Reputational |
| 6. Performance | 12. Dependency |

Figure 7-1: Types of Buyer Risk

1.  **Financial Risk:** Money is always tight for any new purchase. The more an item costs, the higher the associated procurement risk. High project costs also have more people involved in the decision, longer purchase cycles, and increased documentation required to support the purchase. In the back of every buyer's mind is a central question: "How can we minimize the cost and achieve the same business benefit?"

    Also, buyers (especially an Executive Buyer) wants to understand, from the outset, all the costs that will be incurred so no additional funds will be required. If buyers believe that the seller is underestimating costs, fears may arise, and decision making could be halted. The larger the opportunity, the greater the potential risk for a wrong decision.

    Last, no one wants to conduct business with a supplier that is on financial life support.

    **Recommended Action.** Make sure you understand how the buyer measures financial value. CFOs typically use common financial measurement terms such as Return on Investment (ROI), Net Present Value (NPV), Internal Rate of Return (IRR), or Payback. Most of them like to calculate their own metrics or use a neutral third party. Sellers should be careful when discussing financial metrics with a CFO because they often don't trust the information coming from a seller.

If you are asked to calculate financial benefits, be sure you can prove your claim. Examples may include a financial model, third-party endorsement, or verification. Provide alternative options for financing the product or service. Be conversant in the usage of capital asset pricing models that rank different purchases in order of return. Be sure to consider trial periods, gain-sharing, pay per test, subscription pricing, delayed billing, extended warranties, and service support. In complex, high price sales, buyer-centered sellers often include their own CFO or appropriate financial experts in a sales call.

Be able to document your financial health through bank references, credit agencies, or other entities.

2. **Unfamiliarity Risk:** The perception of risk increases when buyers consider making a purchase for the "first time." For many stakeholders, this may be uncharted territory. If the product is new, it helps if the buyer knows you or your company. Buyers gravitate toward established providers and comfortable solutions because the familiarity of the providers makes them feel the "first time" purchase is safe. It is also not unusual for first-time buyers to hire a consultant to help them make the right purchase decision.

   **Recommended Action.** Sell yourself by developing a strong business relationship with all internal and external stakeholders involved in the purchase of your product, service, or solution. Undertake a discovery process that helps you identify the key issues of concern to all stakeholders. Remember, people love to buy, but they hate to be sold. Make it easy for the customer to buy your product or service by providing a list of repeat buyers. You should key in on clients who are respected in the industry. Align executives from your company with their peers in the buying organization. Educate buyers on your company's history, product development successes, test results, firsts in the industry, etc. Then personalize your relationship by making company-sponsored events and site visits to your facility available to them, as well as company testimonials and endorsements, along with industry related white papers that support your proposition.

3. **Personal Risk:** This is important to everyone involved in the process, and it surfaces when the buyer believes that, if they recommend your product, something could go wrong. When people focus on the negative aspects of a pending decision, they begin by asking themselves, "What unpleasant consequences could occur?" "What would be the backlash if the product or project fails to live up to the staff's expectations?" "How will it affect their personal business status and self-esteem?" Once the buyer has evaluated the negative consequences, they can focus on the benefits. "How will this decision impact my personal growth?" "Does it give me recognition?" "Does it provide a future reward?" "Does it solve a critical problem?" "Can it help me achieve my long-term goals and objectives?"

   **Recommended Action.** This takes time and persistence. Develop a list of all the perceived personal risks for each stakeholder and options for them to mitigate risk. Then engage all the stakeholders involved, and explore how risks can be addressed. Consider suggesting a group decision so no one person will receive the credit or the blame. Remember, risk is personal. Remove the personal risk. Be especially careful not to overpromise when you are mitigating personal risks. Conduct a "pilot" or trial of your product for a defined time period with an agreed upon evaluation protocol.

4. **Operational Risk:** Often buyers have concerns over the disruption of supplies or the breakdown of routine operational workflow during a project's implementation. Operational risk could surface in the form of supply delivery and backlog issues, loss or damage to goods in transit, unauthorized increase in the scope of work, or impeded

workflows due to access issues during renovation or construction activities. If work is disrupted, costs will increase, and workers will become frustrated. In the back of everyone's mind is, "How will this new product or project change my day?" Or, "Will the impact be positive or negative?"

**Recommended Action.** To address concerns about disruption of workflow, introduce your implementation plan and your support team. Walk everyone through the process, and develop a checklist of tasks assigned to each stakeholder. Ask for input and offer to customize the plan to match their unique situation. Demonstrate flexibility. Once again, provide a list of customers who will verify that workflow disruptions will be at minimum.

5. **Resource Allocation Risk:** Buyers who are concerned about the availability of resources may raise the following questions:
   - "How much time will it take for everyone to learn the new process or technology or work in the new environment?"
   - "My team is already stretched to the max. How will they react?"
   - "Who will be early adopters? Who will fight the change?"
   - "How will we manage the change and measure competency while still performing normal day-to-day tasks?"
   - "Will the cost of conversion be greater than the measured savings?"

   **Recommended Action.** Change is difficult for most people until they see the benefits. Be sure to engage the customer in the process early and often. Provide a product demonstration, trial period, or evaluation timeline, and use your list to check off the task assignments. Explain and identify your training resources, and provide them with a competency checklist. Make it easy for them to buy from you.

6. **Performance Risk:** New technology is great when it works. "What are the chances of a product recall, inadvertent failure, or early obsolescence?" A product recall costs time and money, and sometimes the

product needs to be replaced with a new supplier. Buyers ask themselves, "Is my risk of product failure high, medium, or low?" "What is the probability of recurring performance issues?" Performance risk includes the seller's ability to meet your purchase order quantities and inventory expectations on time.

**Recommended Action.** With every product, there is always the risk of a product recall or inadvertent failure. The key is to demonstrate that your organization is equipped to "own the issue" with minimal disruption to the customer. Explain your loaner policy, product warranty, service response times, and replacement policy. Describe how you can update software via the internet, etc. Discuss your track record for managing product recalls. To manage orders and inventory expectations, sellers can build and inventory finished goods, add plant capacity, or provide monetary guarantees.

7. **Physical Risk:** Buyers deplore risks to their property, plant, equipment, or personnel. They will ask questions like, "Is the product safe to use in my work environment?" "What are the potential risks to the user?" "Does the product have all of the required federal or agency approvals?"

   **Recommended Action.** If a new product is involved, explain how safety mechanisms have been incorporated into the design of the product based upon extensive customer research. Then explain the extensive testing procedures that are incorporated into the manufacturing process and how they are supported by various regulatory agencies that approve your products. Be sure to describe where the product was tested, and offer investigator contact information. Provide test results from any third party or independent service.

8. **Time Risk:** Time is a vital commodity in business. Buyers want to know the time demands of projects (on themselves and their staff). "How much time do I need to allocate to thoroughly investigate this purchase?" "What questions should I ask?" "Who should I ask?" "Do

I have the time and energy required to conduct this investigation properly?" "Are the time requirements of this project likely to intrude upon other projects of higher priority?"

**Recommended Action.** Organizations often use RFPs for this purpose and often let the vendors educate them. With existing accounts, the best way to minimize this form of risk is through a sound and well-developed account management strategy. You can also mitigate this risk by describing the specific areas that should concern each stakeholder. Let them self-educate, or provide them with a list of their concerns after you have listened and understood their key issues. Why provide a list? Stakeholders can get a list from the web or a third-party testing service. Make it easy for them, and provide it. If your product, service, or solution is best in class, it won't matter. You will stand out!

9. **Risk of Natural Disasters:** Supply chain executives are aware of risks associated with unforeseeable events such as weather, natural disasters, epidemics, port closings, and geopolitical events. They'll want to know, "What natural risks should concern me?" "Can the vendor deliver if a natural disaster occurs?" "Is the seller's strategy for handling natural disasters a sound one?"

   **Recommended Action.** To mitigate concerns about your ability to deliver on time during periods of a natural disaster, describe your contingency plan and the number and location of your manufacturing facilities; provide an example of your on-time delivery report. Explain how your organization has developed a flexible supply chain process that will meet the challenge with a redundant manufacturing capacity that can account for any natural disaster risk situations.

10. **Execution Risk:** This is all about the buyer determining if the vendor can execute the project plan and deliver on time and on budget. "What are the critical factors to success or failure during the planning process? What could go wrong during the implementation phase, and how would we mitigate it?"

**Recommended Action.** You must be able to prove that you can execute the project plan on time and on budget. Every organization has at least one horror story of a project that went over budget, took much more time than expected, or disrupted other vital business activities. Mitigate this risk by sharing your implementation plan and by introducing your implementation team. Share customer testimonials and the results of customers' post implementation surveys. Share what unexpected problems you have had to overcome and how you were able to successfully complete the project. Make them feel comfortable that you will be a responsible, efficient, and suitably flexible project manager.

11. **Reputation Risk:** Buyers always want to protect their organization's reputation. It's important for them to work only with suppliers that will maintain, not tarnish, their image. In the back of their minds, they are always asking the question, "Will this supplier make us look bad and cost us money or business?" Poor quality, repeated product recalls, unethical business practices, and bad press coverage are just a few examples of the risks they'll foresee.

    **Recommended Action.** Sell your image. Provide client references. Invite Procurement and other stakeholders to your organization for a site visit. Provide biographies of your executive leadership, and schedule peer-to-peer meetings. "Walk Your Talk."

12. **Dependency Risk:** Buyers are always careful about being too dependent on a single supplier. They don't want their production to be curtailed, and if they decide to switch suppliers, they don't want a high switching cost.

    **Recommended Action.** This risk is often associated with Procurement. Explain to them how important they are to your organization. Reassure the buyer by explaining you can provide their product from multiple manufacturing facilities located in various countries of the world. Offer to hold some level of their supplies in inventory to cover any potential shortages. Ask about the buyer's supplier relationships and how they have dealt with similar risk.

Risk concerns can arise at any point in the buying process as stakeholders acquire and process information. Consequently, risk mitigation should be a top priority of sellers in all industries throughout the buying process. When building and executing a sales plan, sellers should keep the following points in mind.

### Key Points to Remember for Buyer-Centered Sellers

1. Buyers perceive risk from cognitive factors such as test data, performance records, research reports, internet articles, price, and delivery records.
2. Buyers experience fear from emotional factors such as prior trigger events, stories, events shared by others, and threats to their personal well-being or career.
3. There are twelve major types of buyer risk, but not every risk will be involved in every sale.
4. Identify your buyers' personal risks as well as risks to their business outcomes.
5. Sellers should identify the real or perceived risk for each stakeholder.
6. Stakeholders can categorize risks as high, medium, or low.
7. Sellers should be able to articulate the risk mitigation strategy for each type of risk.
8. The best means for mitigating perceived risk include planning, open and frequent communication with the buying organization, identifying review processes, allocating technical support, and soliciting frontline-user feedback.

## THE SKILL CHALLENGE

In order to become more effective and buyer centered, what is the one thing you will commit to do differently because of reading this chapter? Please write it here or on a separate sheet of paper.

## ADDENDUM 9: RISK ASSESSMENT & MITIGATION WORKSHEET

The Risk Assessment & Mitigation Worksheet can help you identify the twelve major buyer risk categories and the reasons underlying a stakeholder's perceived risk. You can use the worksheet to rank the probability of each risk as high, medium, or low. Finally, you can develop specific risk mitigation strategies for your sales organization. This exercise should be done for every major product or project that you sell. Once completed, share this process with several stakeholders, and get their input.

| Risk Assessment & Mitigation Worksheet | | | | | |
|---|---|---|---|---|---|
| Buyer Risk | Stakeholder & Title | Probability | | | Mitigation Strategy |
| | | High | Medium | Low | |
| Financial | | | | | |
| Unfamiliarity | | | | | |
| Personal | | | | | |
| Operational | | | | | |
| Resource Allocation | | | | | |
| Performance | | | | | |
| Physical | | | | | |
| Time | | | | | |
| Natural Disasters | | | | | |
| Execution | | | | | |
| Reputation | | | | | |
| Dependency | | | | | |

## ADDENDUM 10: HOW "RISK" FACTORS INTO THE VALUE EQUATION FOR STAKEHOLDERS

Risk is a component of every purchase decision. Stakeholders, either individually or collectively, must assess its probability and impact. This Value Equation shows that the Business Impact of a seller's product, service, or solution must exceed the current solution minus the cost to purchase, implement, and use the solution divided by the perceived risks of doing so.

> The combination of measurable business results (KPIs) and the emotional factors that govern them.

> The total costs incurred to achieve the business impact desired.

$$\text{Value} = \frac{\text{Impact (Future State – Current State) – Cost}}{\text{Perceived Risk}}$$

> Real or imagined risks by one or more stakeholders that are involved in the purchase decision.

# Chapter 8

# Cold Case Files: Activating Dormant Leads & Inactive Accounts

"It takes 1–3 touches to reengage an inactive customer."

Jeb Blount—Author of *Fanatical Prospecting*

n 2003 the TV program "Cold Case" had its debut. For the next seven years, the program told the fictional stories of a cold case team and how they navigated the challenges of dealing with witnesses who had evaporated or died and evidence that had been lost or compromised. Since its cancellation, several programs have surfaced that tell similar stories. Perhaps you have seen *Forensic Files* or *Cold Case Files*. Each tells a fascinating story of how persistent detectives and crime scene investigators found new evidence or a new perspective on solving the mystery.

## THE SELLER'S COLD CASES

So how do cold cases tie into dormant leads and inactive accounts? Well, for starters, dormant leads and inactive accounts are a seller's cold cases. They bear many of the same characteristics. Sellers often find that the research conducted six months or a year ago has been lost or misplaced. They know that key influencers were interviewed, but the notes are not in the CRM system. In today's business environment, companies change rapidly. The profile from last year may no longer accurately reflect the interests and concerns of the prospective buyer or "suspect." Executive level changes may have altered the political landscape of the company. Similar to cold case files, dormant leads and inactive accounts may require research, planning, and persistence.

### Story: The McLaren Engineer

On a plane ride from Chicago to Detroit, a friend of ours found himself seated next to a man who was examining pictures, drawings, and diagrams of a McLaren 675LT—a fantastic, rare, and expensive car. When the opportunity arose, our friend asked, "I noticed you were eyeing the McLaren. Are you thinking of buying one?" His seatmate responded by explaining that he had been a design engineer on the McLaren project for more than 10 years. Our friend couldn't contain himself. He asked how the man got involved, how often he test drove the McLaren, the price of the car, etc. When the plane landed and they were preparing to disembark, the automotive engineer said, "You seemed very interested in the 675LT coupe. Would you like for me to connect you with one of our account executives?" Our friend replied, "No, thanks. That car is a little out of my price range."

Actually, it was about $350,000 out of his price range. But he did learn a lesson. Curiosity can be mistaken for interest. The primary difference is that interest implies a relevance to something of importance. Just because you ask questions and show enthusiasm doesn't mean you're a buyer.

---

## The Challenge of Buyer-Centered Selling

*The Buyer's Dilemma:* **Any organization's pursuit of new or expanded revenue streams can suffer from "starts" and "stops" that are maddening and confusing to anyone below the executive level. Buyers and users can be paralyzed by timelines that range from "must do now" to "maybe next quarter" to "whenever."** Internal politics and competing initiatives can turn an exciting project into a "cold case." When support wavers, buyers face a dilemma: should we abort the buying process or continue our research and vetting?

---

*The Seller's Challenge:* **Sellers can strengthen their funnel or pipeline by identifying strong prospects from a list of dormant leads and inactive accounts, and execute a communication strategy that rejuvenates the very best prospects and their projects and initiatives.** By leveraging prior contacts and previous research, a seller may find that a dormant lead or inactive account can be converted into an excellent sales opportunity. By paying attention to dormant leads, sellers may find themselves rediscovering valuable opportunities and can provide the buyer with just what they need—a buyer-centered expert, consultant, and problem solver.

---

In the course of this chapter, we'll explore the differences between dormant leads and inactive accounts, guidelines for evaluating dormant leads, the types of dormant leads, how sellers can get traction from these leads, and how to create and implement an effective communication plan.

## DORMANT LEADS VS. INACTIVE ACCOUNTS

The difference between a dormant lead and an inactive account is likely to change from company to company and industry to industry. Both dormant leads and inactive accounts are:

- Inactive
- Unresponsive
- Don't see themselves as being in the market now

> An inactive or dormant account is a company that made a purchase from you previously (usually within one year) and has not made a purchase with you since that time.

The lead may have originated from a click on your company website, a request for a download, registration on a product website, or through an industry trade show. An inactive or dormant account is a company that made a purchase from you previously (usually within one year) and has not made a purchase with you since that time. A dormant lead is not ready to buy right now but many are likely to buy in the near future. Therefore, it's important to requalify dormant leads.

> A dormant lead is not ready to buy right now but very likely to buy at some point in the future.

Some companies have CRM systems clogged with hundreds of dormant leads and inactive accounts. Senior sales vice presidents across the globe are frustrated with this massive pool of prospects. "What should we do?" "Is there a benefit from pursuing these opportunities?" "Are dormant leads and accounts really a cache of treasures or just discards to be forgotten?"

Most companies establish protocols for judging whether prospects are hot, warm, or cold. Some have a tradition of "passing the torch" to new sellers in hopes that a new team member will discover a solution to an age-old paradox: how do sellers begin a conversation with an unresponsive prospect or account?

Let's take a closer look at dormant leads and inactive accounts—but separately.

### Dormant Leads: Should We Choose Them or Lose Them?

What we do know about lead follow-up is that many sellers—irrespective of the lead's source—fail to respond in a timely fashion. Only 16% of sellers follow up with a meaningful conversation within 24 hours. Sirius Decisions reports that sellers average two attempts to connect with a lead before abandoning their efforts.[1] Yet the average successful sale requires as many as five calls.[2] The data indicates that many sellers are late or give up prematurely when pursuing leads.

Let's examine what research tells us about lead generation and pursuit.

## TEN GUIDELINES FOR UNDERSTANDING THE BUYER

1. **All dormant leads are not the same.** Some leads are not dormant—they are dead! Your job is to create a profile or scorecard that will allow you to distinguish leads that are worth pursuing from those that should be avoided at all cost.

2. **Many dormant leads come back to the market.** John Fakatselis, COO of Accent Technologies, reports that 75% of the leads that don't show firm buying interest at the present time will buy related services inside of 24 months.[3] Buyer-centered sellers perform dormant lead duty.

3. **A prospect's curiosity does not reflect their interest.** Through calls and conversations, buyer-centered sellers distinguish between a lead's curiosity (fascination with a topic) and interest (relevance to a need).

4. **Let your CRM system give you a starting point.** This is the point in your career where you hope your predecessors took better notes than you have. If their records are accurate and provide detailed records of interviews, correspondence, and key points of interest, you may find yourself standing on an excellent launching platform for a new communication campaign.

5. **Investigate the prospect's "footprints" on social media.** Has your prospect posted a profile on LinkedIn? In what groups do they participate? Track their activities. Discover topics of interest. Use Facebook to discover personal interests and activities. Twitter may help you discover possible linkages.

6. **Investigate the prospect's "fingerprints" on your company website.** How did the lead originate? If they clicked on the company website, requested a download, or posted a comment, your lead may be warmer than you think.

7. **A prospect's lack of response may not imply a lack of interest.** Let's suppose that the CRM report showed that you initiated five or six emails during the prior fiscal year but that there were zero responses. Did your message identify a "call to action?" Far too often, we hear stories of prospects who'd received and appreciated messages but were too busy to respond. See if you can catch them at a trade show, event, or conference where you might be able to get a better read on their interest level.

8. **Dormant leads do not belong in your sales funnel.** Dormant leads go "above the funnel" since they need to be requalified.

9. **You can't qualify a dormant lead without contacting your "suspect."** To qualify a prospect, it requires face-to-face or phone-to-phone contact discussing problems the buyer wishes to solve and threats they wish to mitigate or opportunities they wish to pursue.

10. **Qualify, Qualify, Qualify.** Don't waste your time on bad business or impossible "cold cases." Know what you are looking for, and continue to qualify the "suspect."

### Questions to Keep You Buyer Centered

- How did this lead originate?
- What prompted the original contact?
- If this lead were to materialize, would it be worth the effort?
- Why did your lead go dark?
- Where's the competition?
- What changes lead you to believe that these stakeholders are more receptive to change than in the past?
- Who is your lead, and what is their title?
- What do you know about their interests?
- How will they remember you or your company?
- How has the selling landscape into this target organization changed?

- Who can you turn to that would serve as a "confidential informant" and help you understand the political, financial, and decision dynamics?
- What changes in the selling organization (new products, services, test results, etc.) may help you connect your solution to their needs?
- What changes are occurring in their industry (new regulations, mergers, acquisitions) that may help you provide an insight or perspective to generate interest?
- What references can you assemble that may help open the door?
- What insights could you provide that might indicate a problem, opportunity, or threat exists?

## Types of Dormant Leads

There are five types of dormant leads that sellers will encounter.

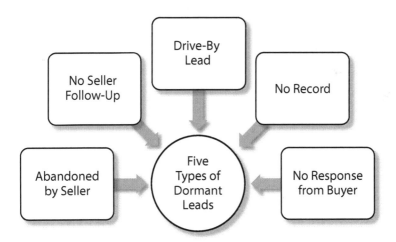

Figure 8-1: Five Types of Dormant Leads Sellers Will Encounter

- **Abandoned by Seller**—you (or your predecessor) determined that the lead was not a qualified source and chose not to respond.

- **No Seller Follow-Up**—you failed to follow up in a timely manner. When you're attempting to balance presentations and proposals with closing important deals, it's easy to lose track of a lead. You transfer a note from the inside sales team to your action list, and then a big deal begins to unravel. A week later, the lead has grown cold.

- **Drive-By Lead**—a prospect visits a trade show booth, clicks on the seller's website, or places a call to the buying organization. You've never known a "drive-by" lead to materialize into a sale, so you ignore the message.

- **No Record**—several members of the selling organization remember a contact, but there is no record of the suspect, form of contact, or dates.

- **No Response from Buyer**—you attempted on one or several occasions to make contact but received no response. "They must not be interested. Just as well—it simplifies my job."

## Inactive Accounts: Are You Getting Traction from Your Action?

Now let's consider dormant or inactive accounts. These are accounts that bought previously from your organization but are no longer purchasing your product, service, or solution. There are subtle but important differences.

Not all inactive accounts are the same. Here are a couple of different types.

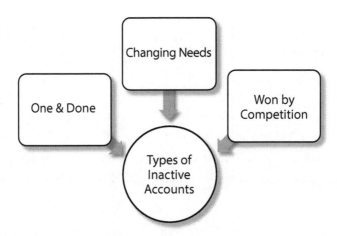

Figure 8-2: Types of Inactive Accounts

- **One & Done**—you sold a product last year that has a life span of five to six years. No additional sales appear possible because of the life span of the product.

### Story: The Farm Equipment Seller

In 2017, a seller sold a Nebraska co-op a John Deere S680 combine for corn and beans for a little more than $340,000. The equipment manager made it clear that their equipment budget did not permit additional purchases in the near future. The seller knew that the S680 combine should last them eight to ten years with proper maintenance. Consequently, the seller removed them from his sales funnel for the foreseeable future. But the seller forgot something very important. He forgot to ask what types of equipment were covered in the equipment budget.

Sometimes companies have equipment budgets for very expensive purchases amortized over many years but have smaller expenditure lines in their annual budget to cover replacements and transport equipment, tarps, and storage equipment. This was a missed opportunity for cross-selling and follow-up conversations. Instead the account went cold.

- **Changing Needs**—Consider the company that stops placing orders with you because their demand has decreased markedly or because they have built up enough inventory to meet the near term anticipated demand.
- **Won by Competition**—The customer chose a different "direction" for one of many reasons: competitive bid, service failure, new product introductions, etc. The seller may have won part but not all of the sales opportunities.

Why pursue inactive accounts? There are several important benefits that may surface as you attempt to qualify an inactive account.

1. Sometimes the data in the CRM system can lead you astray. The information can be out of date or erroneous. Organizations change

quickly, and you may find that this organization's profile, organizational chart, and list of key stakeholders and users may require significant change. A company that you deemed inactive two years ago may be a perfect target today.

2. What's your preferred vendor status? If you sold something to this company, you may find that they perceive you (and your company) as a preferred vendor. Check out your standing with Purchasing or Procurement.

3. Does your customer service or product service team help or hurt you? While you may not have had contact in many months, that doesn't mean your customer service or product service team hasn't had some productive exchanges. Perhaps they have solved a problem or conducted training. Find out what "users" think of your product and company. Their recommendations and experiences could be an excellent launching platform for cross-selling.

4. Do you know the key players on the buyer's side? You may know them (the users and executives), and they may remember you. If so, you may find that the key stakeholders are accessible. That could be a huge time-saver over an account where you are not well connected.

5. Do you have any record of how they make purchasing decisions? A quick review of old files may arm you with an old road map that may come in handy in qualifying this account.

6. Can you make an old sale into a new deal? Are they receptive to a contract renewal, extension, or cross-sell? Remember: you're looking for an opportunity to get on the scoreboard. Times change. A contract renewal may look like a sweet deal.

7. What happened to the competition? One of the great benefits of reenergizing a dormant account is that you will often find that the competition is nowhere to be found. Why would they bird-dog an account that has no sales activity?

## SEVEN LESSONS FROM A COLD CASE TEAM

Short of spending the next several weeks viewing old episodes of *Forensic Files*, here are seven lessons that many top performers learned from their careful review of dormant leads and inactive accounts.

1. Successful cold case teams develop a profile or scorecard of a good cold case and rigorously apply the criteria in determining which cases to pursue and which to abandon.

   **Recommended Action:** Sellers should build a scorecard and avoid wasting time on dead or unqualified leads.

2. Homicide units conduct cold case reviews several times a year.

   **Recommended Action:** Sellers should make a list of dormant leads and inactive accounts and review them quarterly. Look for the one or two jewels that will save you time and position you well with stakeholders.

3. Homicide units look for technological breakthroughs that may cast new light on an investigation.

   **Recommended Action:** Sellers may find sales analytics helpful, especially if it incorporates artificial intelligence in assessing quality leads, while social media may aid in researching and connecting with prospects.

4. Great cold case teams are persistent in collecting new evidence and recording new information and insight in the "murder book." A murder book is the case file for the murder investigation and may include forensic reports, photographs, interview notes, sketches.

   **Recommended Action:** A seller's "murder book" is the CRM file. Make sure everything that might be relevant in the future is recorded.

5. Successful cold case teams contact and interview family members, witnesses, and suspects.

   **Recommended Action:** Sellers should take a similar approach and plan interviews with users (of your solution), proponents, and executive decision makers.

6. Apply the appropriate statute of limitations.

   **Recommended Action:** For many sellers, a lead that is more than a week old may be dead or diminished. In some industries, sales teams apply a six-month benchmark before classifying an account as "inactive." Determine the statute of limitations, and respect the timelines.

7. Build a case that the District Attorney (DA) can take to trial.

   **Recommended Action:** For sellers, the challenge is to build a case that qualifies the lead or account as a viable prospect that can be repositioned from "above the funnel" to "in the funnel." Your "DA" is your sales manager.

## BUILDING A BUYER-CENTERED COMMUNICATION PLAN

If you have reviewed your list of dormant leads and inactive accounts, it's now time to build a communication plan that will drive buying activity.

- **Set realistic expectations for dormant leads.** Don't anticipate an immediate response. Don't expect too much, too quickly, or too often. Buyer-centered sellers are in it for the long run.

### Story: "The Long Run"

Kelly, a commercial realtor in a tough market in the Midwest, is a great example of a buyer-centered seller. Sharon, a VP of operations for a manufacturing company in Omaha, NE, is the embodiment of a dormant lead. Sharon first contacted Kelly a year-and-a-half ago, when her company was considering an expansion of their corporate headquarters. Kelly helped Sharon grasp the financial intricacies of the commercial real estate market in Omaha. Kelly organized briefings for Sharon's team and developed several hypothetical scenarios to guide her decision process. Suddenly, Sharon stopped returning her calls. But Kelly had been following the companies in the Midwest and knew this was a difficult time, especially for manufacturing. Many companies were outsourcing their manufacturing to Asia, where labor costs were lower. But Kelly persisted with emails, voice messages, and texts. She sent periodic reports to Sharon on how artificial intelligence and robotics were helping companies in the manufacturing sector defray costs.

Then one day Kelly's cell phone rang, and it was Sharon. "Kelly, I wanted to catch up with you and apologize for the long silence. It has taken us a while to crawl out of a dark financial hole. But I think we're on solid ground. Your emails, especially the ones on AI, helped immensely. They pushed our thinking in the right direction. Just this week we have been able to recapture a couple of accounts that we had lost to manufacturers in Indonesia. If you have time, I'd like to resume our discussions on commercial sites. Our needs have changed quite a bit, but you're the only one I trust to guide our decision making."

Buyer-centered sellers are in it for the long run.

- **Apply a scorecard composed of key criteria to identify the strongest prospects.** Verify information about the company and your prospective buyers, and have faith in your scorecard criteria.

- **Review all relevant CRM files.** Make sure that you debrief with prior sales representatives and account managers. They may be able to offer insight into why the account went "dark" and what steps NOT to take.

- **Choose content that provokes or offers insight.** Establish yourself as an experienced problem solver…not a seller. Don't sell—educate!

- **Craft a compelling value message designed for different types of stakeholders.** Check with other sellers to identify content that has appeal.

- **Plan periodic messages that create awareness.** It's difficult to establish awareness in two or three messages. Be persistent.

- **Personalize your messages.** Check out your lead on social media, and gather information that will help you personalize your messages. Relevant personalized messages drive 18 times more revenue than broadcast emails.[4]

- **If you have sold something in the past, use a service call as a conversation starter.** While they may not be interested in buying…it's likely that they are interested in performance and service.

- **Search for social media affiliations.** Create alerts on social media to signal a prospect's contributions.

- **Automate your detection.** Social media often provide "alerts" that help you identify a prospect's activity quickly.

- **Find a referral for every dormant lead.** The most reliable way to connect with a prospect is through a respected referral. Who do you know that they are likely to respect?

- **Uncover new witnesses.** Over the course of six to twelve months, many factors may change. Look for new stakeholders, new political alliances, and a larger group of users who were unknown or silent in the past.

### Key Points to Remember for Buyer-Centered Sellers

Consider these key points as you review your dormant leads and inactive accounts.

1. A dormant lead and inactive account share common features; they are inactive, unresponsive, and see themselves as "not in the market."

2. Some dormant leads are dead—choose carefully, or you will waste valuable time.

3. Many dormant leads return to the market and make a related purchase within 24 months. Buyer-centered sellers maintain contact and open lines of communication with stakeholders.

4. Check to see if your prospect is interested (sees the topic as relevant to their needs) or just curious (fascinated with the topics).

5. Track your prospects on social media to discover interests and activities.

6. Dormant leads should not be in your sales funnel.

7. It's vital that you qualify your leads continuously through the reactivation process.

8. There are different types of dormant leads, ranging from abandoned by the seller to unresponsive buyers.

9. There are several reasons for pursuing a dormant account; you may have sold a product or service and know the players and the buying process.

10. Dormant accounts—ones in which you have sold a product or service—may serve as a great launching platform for cross-selling.

11. In launching a communication campaign to rejuvenate a dormant account, be sure to set realistic expectations, scorecard accounts to identify the best prospects, craft content that offers insight, and find a referral that will open the door.

12. The goal for dormant leads and inactive accounts is to create a sales opportunity that can be placed into a sales funnel.

## THE SKILL CHALLENGE

In order to become more effective and buyer centered, what skill can you identify from the content in this chapter that requires skill and practice? Please write it here or on a separate sheet of paper.

_____

_____

_____

_____

_____

_____

# Chapter 9

# Unlocking the Executive Mindset: Selling Up

"Focus on what matters (to them). Dig deep. Talk the language and metrics that matter to your executive buyer."

Mike Kunkle—Sales Transformation Specialist

Gaining an audience with a senior executive seems to be on every seller's to-do list. The assumption is that, if they can get 30 minutes of a senior executive's time, something magical will happen. Perhaps the executive will be so impressed with the meeting that he/she will override a committee's deliberation and mandate a decision in the seller's favor. Or perhaps the executive will issue a purchase order or write out a three-year contract for the seller's services. Of course, it's foolishness to believe that any of this is likely to happen quickly or as the result of a single meeting or conversation.

Unfortunately, we've developed an obsession with "selling to the top." The old axiom, "Sell high, wide, and deep," has been rewritten as "Sell high." Many sales managers admit to pushing their frontline team to get as high as possible with little or no consideration of risk/reward and without proper preparation or coaching. The challenge facing the seller is to determine who from the buying organization can make an impact on the buying process or decision, when contact would be most beneficial, and how an executive would benefit from a meeting with the seller.

### Story: The Director of Endowment & Gifts

Joann is the Director of Endowment & Gifts for the Museum of Southwestern Art (MSA) in Albuquerque, NM. MSA is an independent, non-profit museum that specializes in collecting and conserving paintings, pottery, textiles, and paper artifacts that convey the history of the southwestern United States. MSA depends on gifts and contributions from businesses, patrons, and benefactors to operate and expand the museum's cultural activities and specialty exhibits.

MSA has launched a new capital campaign designed to increase their endowment by $30M. Joann's responsibility is to drive contributions. In particular, her challenge is to work closely with a small group of "platinum-level members," who pledge more than $100,000 annually.

Bill is a wealthy contributor whose wife, Justine, is very engaged in a wide spectrum of charities in the greater Albuquerque community. In the past, Bill has been generous and responsive to the needs of the MSA, but several "red flags" have surfaced and have Joann concerned. Bill and Justine did not attend the recent "kickoff" dinner for the capital campaign. Bill did not return his pledge card and has not responded to Joann's phone calls. Further, at a recent networking social hour, Joann heard that Justine was focusing her charitable efforts on educational programs for students in K-12. Taken together, these "red flags" might indicate a shift in Bill's contributions. Joann began developing a plan.

### Unknowns:

— Has Justine's interest in K-12 programs influenced Bill's support for MSA?

— Is Justine aware of MSA's programs with K-12?

— Are other interests influencing Bill's charitable giving efforts?

— Who at (MSA) knows someone who also knows Justine well and can promote contact?

— What kind of "win" is Justine seeking from her sponsorship of K-12 programs?

— How do Bill and Justine make decisions regarding gifts and contributions?

### Research Plans:

— Research Justine's involvement in K-12 programs.

— Identify MSA's patrons and "platinum-level members" who might know Justine.

— Prepare a "brief" on MSA's educational events and activities for K-12.

### Key Action Steps:

— Get to Bill and familiarize him with the broad scope of education programs provided by MSA.

— Engage Justine through an on-site tour of MSA with details on education activities that "touch" K-12 students.

— Enlist Justine's efforts for molding and expanding the interface between K-12 and MSA. Change her perspective by helping her see MSA as another "educational institution" that can bring "alive" the history of the southwest to students of all ages.

— Identify members of the MSA board who are well connected with the K-12 community, including former teachers, administrators, and elected officials.

— Explore Bill and Justine's interest in "naming" a Family exhibit created for the K-12 community in Albuquerque.

To many readers, Joann's job may not appear to be that of a sales professional. On the contrary, endowment executives are shouldered with one of the most challenging positions in our career field. Contributors (buyers) can afford donations to a wide spectrum of charities. If one charity is suspect for any reason, the contributor can simply move their donation to another, more deserving, fund. Unlike more traditional sellers, endowment executives sell membership, community enhancement, enrichment of the arts, etc. Every contributor's perception of value is different. If you think this isn't a complex sale, try to calculate the ROI on membership.

---

## The Challenge of Buyer-Centered Selling

***The Buyer's Dilemma:* Buyers are looking for road maps and experienced guides who can help them anticipate and resolve problems while reaping benefits of timely and affordable change.** Most executives harbor a deep-seated concern for three business factors: the power of their brand, revenue growth, and customer loyalty.

***The Seller's Challenge:* Buyer-centered sellers focus on unlocking the executive "mindset" by addressing business issues with a combination of insight and experience that lays the foundation for mutually beneficial commitments and receptivity to change.** This means understanding when it's necessary to connect, how executive level conversations are unique, and what insight and selling skills may be tested during the conversation or meeting.

---

"Executive" is a term that varies widely across industries and companies in its meaning. The "Executive Buyer" is a phrase we use to identify the executive who "owns" the project and funding for a purchase. Executive Buyers have the authority to approve a purchase or stop a buying process. They are the final "yes." Executive Buyers may have innocuous titles like "director," "manager," or "team lead," while others are "president," "vice-presidents" or "chief officers." In some cases, the authority to buy may be delegated to a committee or group.

In this chapter, we'll explore answers to the following questions and aid the seller in developing a buyer-centered approach that unlocks the executive mindset.

- Who is the executive responsible for addressing the problem, pursuing the opportunity, or mitigating the threat (POT) that the seller can impact?

- What factors should sellers consider when determining whether an executive conversation is necessary or mutually beneficial?
- Why has it become necessary for many sales professionals who have sold successfully at a lower level in the customer's organization to connect with the executive team?
- How is an executive level conversation or sales call different from more traditional mid-level sales calls?
- What are the keys to connecting with the executive mindset?
- What preparatory steps should sellers take to become confident and ready to sell at the executive level?
- What are the seven lethal mistakes sellers make when preparing for executive conversations?
- How can sellers build credibility and deliver value in a conversation?
- What research tools are available to provide insight into an executive's mindset?
- What is a realistic outcome for the meeting?

## IS AN EXECUTIVE LEVEL CONVERSATION THE RIGHT STEP TO TAKE?

### Deciding Whether to Pursue an Executive Conversation

At times, sellers ignore the significant downside risk at the executive level. All too often, the seller is unprepared for the executive's questions, can't provide a compelling reason for change, or doesn't understand fully where the executive is in the buying process. Before you press the "up" button on the elevator, you may want to ask yourself some questions that will help you determine whether the elevator ride is necessary and appropriate. "Should I stay, or should I go?"

- Is this executive the Executive Buyer for my sales opportunity?
- Is this an appropriate point in the buying process for an executive conversation?
- Am I the best representative from my company for this level of contact?

- Do I have insight or experience to share that will connect with larger corporate initiatives like revenue growth, customer loyalty, or brand identity?
- Am I ready for tough questions?
- Have I fully researched this executive, and do I understand his/her issues, challenges, and terminology?
- Have I reviewed the professional background of the executive?
- Is there anyone at the executive level in the buying organization that I can leverage for support?
- Do I know how to conduct a strategic conversation?

If your answer is "no" to a few of these questions, you may want to rethink your game plan. Perhaps an executive from your company might be a better fit for the sales call. If your product is a commodity, you may be better positioned if you focus on stakeholders closer to the decision process.

There is a significant upside if your executive is "in the club" and knows how to converse strategically. The downside is executive ego; your executive can blow the deal, may not connect, and may "black hole" your involvement.

Let's consider some "tipping points" (factors that might warrant an executive conversation) and "sticking points" (factors that might preclude an executive conversation).

## Tipping Points

Several factors may justify an executive conversation.

- This executive is the Executive Buyer for one or more of the products or services in the seller's portfolio.
- The seller's company has resources, capabilities, or experience that may be of value to an Executive Buyer who is driving a high priority initiative.
- The seller has secured an executive referral or introduction.
- The seller is an account manager with a sizeable product or service "footprint" in the buying organization and is perceived as a trusted advisor.

## Sticking Points

There are several conditions that should cause a seller to re-evaluate a decision to seek an executive conversation.

- The seller's product is perceived industry-wide to be a commodity.
- The target executive is not "copied" on committee reports and meeting summaries.
- The executive has either a "hands off" approach or zero involvement in the decision process. Some Executive Buyers prefer to push the decision process down the corporate ladder to the appropriate level in their organization.

## Why Are Executive Level Connections Becoming More Critical?

In large measure, there has been a redefinition of the Executive Buyer's role in purchasing. You may judge for yourself the applicability of an executive's role to your specific market and product portfolio.

Figure 9-1: Why Executive Level Connections Are Becoming More Critical

- **Formalized Buying Processes.** Many organizations are redefining their buying processes to drive out unnecessary cost. They are centralizing decision-making authority at a high level, often relegating the role of Strategic Procurement to the executive level. For the seller this is a double-edged sword. Some Procurement leaders buy outcomes and will pay a fair price. Others view your product or service as a commodity and drive down price relentlessly.

- **Decision by Consensus.** On the other hand, the senior management team in many organizations relies on consensus-driven groups and assessment committees for product comparisons and decisions. Without a clear preference from a senior executive, many purchasing decisions become stalled or default to an existing supplier.

- **Executive Guidance.** Due to the sheer volume of purchasing requirements, committees now look to their executive sponsors (those who are tasked with addressing the problem, opportunity, or threat) for guidance to prioritize projects and develop a decision-tree analysis based on the needs/demands of the division or organization. In many industries, decision-making has been delegated to Procurement due to volume and expertise. Executives are becoming increasingly involved in Procurement reform because their needs are better met through a different organizational model.

- **Enterprise Solutions.** Many sellers are finding themselves faced with selling a broad scope of products and/or services. While one product may apply to a single division or silo of a buying organization, other products in their portfolio may have enterprise-wide appeal. This may necessitate selling to a senior executive who holds a greater span of authority across many divisions.

- **Strategic Partnerships.** These alliances may underscore interests that are aligned with a common goal among senior stakeholders.

### How Is an Executive Level Conversation Unique?

Let's begin by understanding that a senior executive's expectations for the conversation or sales call are buyer-centered. Executives are hopeful that the seller will bring to the discussion (at minimum) four key contributions: industry experience, understanding of the customer's business model, an awareness of corporate level priorities and initiatives, and a focus on resolving their issues and addressing their needs.

An executive will value a sales call if they feel they received a gift from the seller in the process. The gift is one of knowledge, industry insights, regional or local market trends, etc. Executives value sellers who share insight and expand their scope of understanding. Insight and experience can be a powerful gift that justifies additional conversation. You now have the beginning of a trusted advisor relationship.

In 2014, Forrester Research Inc. published the results of a study focused on uncovering executive expectations[1]. Forrester asked 319 executive-level buyers whether their experience showed that sellers were prepared for meetings. Results revealed a significant gap between executive expectations and seller preparedness.

Let's look at the degree to which executive-level buyers felt their expectations were met in five specific areas: Forrester asked if sellers had:

- "Knowledge about my industry." 58% said "No."
- "Knowledge about my specific business." 76% said "No."
- Shown proof the seller was able to "Understand my issues and where they can help." 78% said "No."
- "Prepared for the questions that I ask." 70% said "No."
- "Relevant examples or case studies to share with me." 79% said "No."

Figure 9-2: Four Key Contributions Executives Perceive Lacking

Forrester's report eloquently summarizes the situation. The majority of Executive Buyers perceive sellers as lacking sufficient:

- Knowledge of the industry or specific business
- Understanding of their challenges and initiatives
- Preparation to answer key questions
- Relevant examples and case studies

"What's surprising is that sales representatives aren't better prepared to create value for buyers during these precious opportunities. For example, salespeople who can communicate only in terms of products and services will see their message resonate with Procurement-level buyers, but they will fail to hit the mark with executives."[2]

If you want to connect at the executive level (and successfully enhance your prospects of winning a complex sale) you'll need to elevate your game. You will need to develop a call plan that is buyer centered and relevant to critical corporate goals like revenue growth and brand identity. You will want to scorecard yourself by answering the following questions:

- "How can I best demonstrate my knowledge and experience in the customer's industry without telling a prospect what they already know?"

- "What business issues are likely to be 'top of mind' to my Executive Buyer?"
- "What metrics will my product or solution positively impact?"
- "How can I quantify value and not just compare products?"
- "How can I become an 'active listener' during our conversation so that I demonstrate a laser-like focus on my customer's issues and priorities?"

## HOW RESEARCH CAN UNLOCK AN EXECUTIVE'S MINDSET

There is a growing box of tools that can help sellers better understand their executive target and develop a call plan that is buyer centered. In fact, the internet is so rich in blogs, articles, and financial reports that it's almost overwhelming. Sellers may find it helpful to focus and narrow their research on specific questions. Consider these questions as a starting guide for developing a knowledge base for an executive conversation.

### Questions to Guide a Seller's Preparation

- What industry headwinds and/or tailwinds is this customer facing?
- Who are your customer's competitors, and how are they performing?
- What are the top three challenges or initiatives this executive is facing?
- How is the buying organization performing from a financial perspective?
- What cost factors are challenging this organization and industry?
- What challenges face the buying organization as they serve their customers?
- What function or role does this executive play in the buying process?
- What new revenue stream is the buying organization pursuing?
- What KPIs are most likely to resonate with the executive?
- What experience does your executive have with your proposed solutions?
- Who in the buying organization will your executive turn to for insight, support, or guidance?
- Why is this the right time for an executive call?
- Where is the buying organization in the buying process?

- How autonomous or collaborative are the decision processes in the buying organization?
- Has there been turnover in the executive ranks? Is the executive new or established?

While strong industry and business knowledge can be very helpful in planning an executive level conversation, focus your research and preparation on crafting a response to the following questions; they are likely to occupy the thoughts of an executive during their conversation with you.

Figure 9-3: Five Questions Executives Ask Themselves

**"Why Am I Here?"** Give some thought to crafting a powerful statement of focus for the meeting (a "focused opening") that answers the question, "Why is this executive investing precious time with me?"

**"Do You Understand My Issues?"** With your knowledge of their challenges or obstacles—along with an acute awareness of current market forces impacting your customer's business—how will you demonstrate your knowledge of their industry and business?

**"What's My Win?"** How will you focus on their business benefit and document real value? How does this product drive change that supports key executive-level initiatives? How does your product deliver personal value to the executive (for example, esteem, recognition, career enhancement)?

**"Why You?"** How can you differentiate your product or yourself without bashing the competition? Do the differences matter to your executive? If you differentiate your solution from the competition by showing its relevance, uniqueness, and urgency, you will deliver a powerful message.

**"OK, What's Next?"** Last, what step(s) must the executive take to realize the full benefits promised in your conversation? If you can't get your customer to move the buying process forward, everything you thought you accomplished will be at risk. Also, remember that planned action by both parties provides an excellent platform for advancing the buying process.

Plan your answers to these basic questions many Executive Buyers ask:

- What's the benefit for me personally?
- What's my ROI? Remember, this is usually measured in financial terms but could encompass non-financial criteria.
- How's this product/solution different from what we've got now?
- How's this product/solution different from the competition?
- What proof do you have for your claim?
- Who on your client list can I call?
- What's your experience in my industry?
- Who's responsible if something goes wrong?
- Why do we have to make this decision now?
- What steps have you taken to make sure nothing goes wrong?
- Making this decision could be a real challenge. How can you help us get on the same page and make a collaborative decision?
- What potential risks am I facing and how will you help prevent or mitigate these challenges?

### Draw from a Broad Base of Research Tools

Many research tools are widely known in the selling profession but not widely used or understood. Hoover's and InsideView are "market intelligence brokers." They provide an excellent tool for capturing a company's profile or gaining an overview of a company's financial performance. Also, they can provide employee information, lists of competitors, and information about product development and releases.

Most company websites will have the latest bios on the executive team and provide useful investor information, including K-10 reports. Avention's

OneStop (now owned by DNB Hoovers or DNB.com) subscription includes financial reports, SWOT analyses, and industry reports. Some sellers use Google Alerts for immediate updates related to a customer or follow other internet alerts. You might consider *FirstRain,* which is another service.

LinkedIn is more than a list of professional associates. Learn to use LinkedIn to "follow" companies and individuals. Capture what industry leaders are saying about the market, their customers, and their products. Don't just build a network—use your connections as referrals and champions who attest to your claims and capabilities.

Sellers often under-utilize the opportunities afforded by trade shows and conferences. Our recommendation is that sellers get out of the booth and find their executive prospects. They should create a list of "targets" for each trade show. Are any target executives presenting papers or participating on panels? Are target executives likely to attend the opening reception or the closing dinner? Will they respond to an invitation to lunch? Will current customers provide an introduction? A trade show, conference, or exhibition affords the seller an opportunity to connect with executives when their schedules are fluid and open to change.

Many companies are turning to "executive briefings"—either in the form of open webcasts or meetings customized for the attending companies. They provide a great opportunity to focus on issues instead of products. The benefits are mutual. They allow the potential customer to answer questions that have surfaced during internal discussions, and the seller's organization can better understand customer needs.

Interviews with former employees or consultants can be especially helpful in filling gaps about who's really in charge, how executives make decisions, and which direct reports they consult to make purchasing decisions.

Twitter—This platform is very popular for many professionals. During trade shows, speakers and executives will often Tweet and re-Tweet others.

You Tube—Speakers and other executives often have speeches and other events posted.

# HOW BUYER-CENTERED SELLERS AVOID POTHOLES, BARRIERS, AND OBSTACLES

A lot has been written about the value of asking good questions during a sales call. Questions can prompt the buyer's participation and allow a seller to gain reliable information. However, we've met our share of sellers who blend a toxic mix of bad questions with poor timing and then wonder why the buyer tuned out halfway through the call.

## Six Mistakes to Avoid When Conversing With an Executive

1.  **Not asking permission to raise questions.** In Neil Rackham's *Spin Selling*[3], he points out that, by asking for permission, the seller establishes an expectation for how the conversation will proceed.

2.  **Asking for information that the seller should already know.** Executives expect a high level of readiness from sellers. If a seller starts asking questions that should have been researched, it indicates that the seller is unprepared and unlikely to have the knowledge and skill to provide help. Every question makes a statement about the seller's readiness. Executives begin to tune out a seller who asks for "background" or "public" information. Bad questions can lead to a loss of credibility. This can be a killer and reflects poor planning, lack of due diligence, and a general disinterest in the executive's business.

3.  **Asking questions that don't lead the buyer to discover or explore a possibility.** The seller's objective should be to help the executive identify problems, opportunities, threats, resources, or solutions. Buyer-centered sellers craft questions to increase the executive's understanding. For example, a seller might ask, "If something were to go wrong with the current software program, what's the backup plan?" Ask questions where the answer doesn't really matter. It's more about getting the executive to think about your point.

4.  **Not asking follow-up questions that drill down on a key point.** If the seller determines that the executive has a problem, the seller may

wish to pose a series of follow-up questions that explore the problem's size, scope, urgency, cause and implications.

5. **Asking detailed questions too soon in the conversation.** It's hard to keep a focus on broad issues when the conversation has re-focused on details. Often executives begin to lose interest and the conversation slows to a stop. Buyer-centered sellers win deals on broad issues, not details.

6. **Not establishing a connection between the seller's solution and the executive's problem, opportunity, or threat.** The seller's questions need to uncover a link that helps the executive see value in the context of other challenges and opportunities. For example, a question may uncover a problem in the continuous delivery of critical materials by the current supplier. If the seller wants to establish a connection between the problem and a solution, the seller may wish to say, "This is a continuing problem for many manufacturers. Later, I can share with you our experience in technologically enhanced supply systems that can help you correct the problem quickly." Buyer-centered sellers are careful to share their solution or set an appointment for quick follow-up.

## Seven Lethal Mistakes to Avoid When Planning Executive Conversations

1. **No Focus.** Sellers can't expect all executives to know how or why someone got on their calendar or remember the gist of a phone call two weeks ago. Many sellers begin the conversation as if they were a "talking brochure." It sounds like what it is—a "product pitch."

   **Recommended Action:** Sellers should begin the meeting with a quick refresher of the reason for the meeting and the benefit the executive can expect. Keep the message simple, direct, and positive. Use it to leverage yourself into the conversation.

2.  **Got a Time Slot? Think Again!** Just because a seller has been granted a thirty-minute appointment on an executive's calendar doesn't mean things will work out as planned. It's easy to find the time slot compromised by phone calls, overly long meetings, emergencies, or travel time from locale to locale.

    **Recommended Action:** Sellers need to plan two "on the run" adjustments: a) if the meeting starts late and b) if the meeting ends abruptly. For example, when a conversation ends abruptly for any reason, a seller should consider asking permission to reschedule with his/her assistant to complete the discussion. If the meeting is delayed, plan a three- or four-minute "teaser" that will pique their interest without whittling down the content. Then ask for a new meeting slot to address the full value of the message.

3.  **Too Much Detail.** Many executives have a "big picture" perspective on situations. Seldom are they willing to wade through details to understand your product or solution.

    **Recommended Action:** Sellers should be careful to craft a headline. Develop a "sound bite" to convey a macro view of the problem, opportunity, threat, the implications, and benefits. Clearly define the current state and the future state, the gap, its cause, and the cost of inaction. Anticipate one or two questions that might arise about any key points. Expect executives to question your claims; be ready with evidence, case studies, and testimonials. When using PowerPoint, sellers should limit the number of slides; keep the slides simple; resist telling everything you know. Consider using a "placemat" that illustrates the points you wish to make. It's high-level, original, and successful with executives because it gets them engaged.

4.  **Too Many Questions.** Most call plan methodologies encourage the seller to raise questions for a couple of reasons. First, questions get the executive involved in the conversation and prevent the seller from delivering a boring monologue that is often referred to as "the pitch."

Second, questions often provide sellers with the answers they need to develop an effective sales strategy. However, those same questions may do little to benefit the executive.

**Recommended Action:** Sellers should craft three or four questions that will help the executive consider the scope of the opportunity or problem and the implications of failing to address the situation quickly. Buyer-centered sellers have a specific objective in mind when crafting questions, like heightening a sense of urgency or recognizing the unidentified costs of the current state or situation. A good question makes the executive pause, think, and reflect. If they respond with a comment like "That's a great question. I need to think about that," then you know you have hit a home run and established credibility. These become "foundation questions." Sellers should "get to the point." If the buyer feels there are too many questions, they may not see the seller's value. Get to the point quickly.

5.  **No Relevance.** Many sellers become so product focused that they forget to link their product or service to a C-level initiative. Executives often see their responsibilities as champions of multiple corporate initiatives. One executive explained that, "It's like driving several busses to different destinations with different departure and arrival schedules. First, I need to figure out which bus trip is most immediate, affordable, and achievable. Second, I need to get everyone on board. Last, I have to figure out what to do about the rest of my trips."

    **Recommended Action:** Sellers must establish a link between their product or service and some initiative that's relevant to their executive. They make sure they have support for their claim, including case studies, testimonials, referrals, and/or a business case. Sellers should be ready for "drill down" questions associated with their documentation.

6.  **Don't Know "C-Speak."** Often sellers find they don't seem to "speak the same language" as the executive. A common language can bring two people together. Differences in language can drive them apart.

**Recommended Action:** Savvy sellers get coaching on key terms used by executives in the buying organization. What terms or phrases do they use to label their business concerns or challenges? How do they describe high priority initiatives? What are their "pet phrases?" What is the correct industry jargon? There is a big difference between "Innovative Procurement" and "Procuring for Innovation."

7. **Forgot the Next Step.** Relationships—whether professional or social—are built over the course of many conversations. Each conversation should create a "bridge" to the next while building on the relationship.

   **Recommended Action:** Sellers must establish a need for a subsequent conversation, meeting, or presentation. This means identifying a benefit or deliverable that will justify a next step in the eyes of the executive. While it may be difficult to calculate the course of the initial conversation in advance, our recommendation is that no seller leave the room without identifying the value a subsequent conversation would provide. Sellers should make sure the "next step" aligns with the course of the buying process.

## Seven Tough Conversation-Stoppers

An essential step in becoming "executive ready" is to anticipate tough questions and concerns that can derail a conversation. In our experience with sellers from different industries, there are (at least) seven comments or questions that often surface at some juncture in the conversation.

1. **"Good is good enough."** What the executive may be saying is, "I don't need great. Good will do just fine. In fact, I can't afford great." The seller's challenge is to identify a benefit that justifies change and uncovers the conditions under which "good" becomes outdated, costly, and ineffective.

2. **"What does this have to do with me?"** What the executive may be asking is, "I don't understand the relevance this product has for the initiatives that are hounding me 24/7." The seller's challenge is to draw a strong connection between the product/solution and a significant

corporate initiative. Sellers have to move beyond what the product "is" and focus the executive conversation on what the product "does" and how it benefits the organization.

3. **"This sounds far too complicated."** What the executive may be saying is, "I don't have the time or interest in managing this project to completion. I've got bigger (or more immediate) issues on my plate." The seller's challenge is to offer a "road map" or implementation plan along with the expertise to ensure completion of the project. You may want to simplify your message. You could be providing too many details to a strategic minded person.

4. **"How does this move the needle?"** What the executive may be asking is, "What measurable benefits will I see, and when do I get the payoff from my investment?" The seller's challenge is to document ROI and offer confirmation such as case studies, test results, business cases, and testimonials.

5. **"We're just not ready for this now."** What the executive may be saying is, "We don't handle change well." The seller's challenge is to provide a game plan, technical expertise, and project management skills to effect change. The executive wants to know that the seller understands the buying culture and how to achieve consensus in an organization that resists change.

6. **"We're happy with what we've got."** What the executive may be saying is, "We know the present solution isn't a long-term 'fix,' but it's not broken." The seller's challenge is to quantify the "cost of inactivity." Sellers need to push the "panic button" and help executives see the risk and downside of not changing soon. Sellers should carefully describe the cost of inaction. Define specifically the difference between the current state and the future state. Clearly articulate the pain of not acting.

7. **"Too much risk."** What the executive may be saying is, "It seems like every time we make a change, something goes wrong, and I've

been left picking up the pieces." The seller's challenge is to outline a comprehensive risk mitigation plan. This means understanding risk from the executive's perspective.

## HOW BUYER-CENTERED SELLERS BECOME THE IDEAL SELLER

Every conversation with an executive should form an impression for the executive—about the seller, the product/solution, and the selling organization. The ideal seller crafts each conversation to portray a powerful image that differentiates the seller from the competition and reveals the seller as a valued, helpful advisor. The ideal image will differ from seller to seller, depending on industries, organizational cultures, and customers. Sellers must research, plan, and rehearse to become effective in conveying the intended image. For many of our friends and colleagues in this profession, there are three core elements to the image they wish to portray.

- The seller is a change management specialist with extensive industry experience who understands the executive's business model, culture, initiatives, and priorities.

- The seller is a solution provider who offers a product/solution that supports and enables the pursuit of key corporate-level objectives with measurable benefits that have been demonstrated with other customers.

- The seller converses as an equal who helps Executive Buyers understand problems, navigate challenges, and overcome obstacles.

### Build Your Credibility Around Seven Key Deliverables

Sellers often forget that value isn't just what a product does for a customer; it's about what the seller can do for the executive to simplify, clarify, and strengthen the validity of the buying process. Consider seven key deliverables that sellers can provide and which executives may not get from internal sources.

Figure 9-4: Seven Key Deliverables Sellers Should Provide

1. **Uncover Hidden Problems.** Many buying organizations have an uncanny ability to overlook, ignore, or disguise problems. However, sellers have the advantage of a broad perspective of companies. Most executives welcome an independent and unbiased view of the situation. Sellers can help an executive by sharing experiences with other customers. In many regards, the seller can act as an outside consultant.

2. **Identify Key Resources.** Sometimes the resources required to solve a problem may not be immediately apparent. Sellers need to overcome viewing their role as a "product provider" and think of how they can serve as a broker of resources. Necessary resources may lie in the seller's organization or with third parties. How can sellers use their knowledge of other buying organizations to help the executive buy?

3. **Build Internal Consensus.** More executives are insisting on internal collaboration (and, ultimately, consensus) as a foundation for important

purchasing decisions. Sellers can add value by working with each committee member or buyer to share perspectives held by other buyers. Sellers can create the consensus that the executive requires. This is a critical role when faced with selling into silos in complex organizations.

4. **Quantify & Document Value.** Too often we have seen situations where sellers left Procurement with the responsibility of building a business case, quantifying a benefit, or documenting value. That's a very bad idea! Ask the executive to identify "key performance indicators" or value measures. Then offer to develop an initial draft of a business case. The solution should provide value that will be a win for both the seller and the executive.

5. **Identify Hidden Costs & Risks.** Often, we find members of the buying team who are prone to ignore costs and risks associated with a current supplier or an internally harvested solution. Sellers would do well to take a fresh look at the "hard" and "soft" costs, benefits, and risks of the current solution. At the very least, a seller should offer to share a professional cost comparison with the executive that clearly shows the cost of inaction.

6. **Capture an Opportunity or Competitive Advantage.** To identify or capture a competitive advantage, the seller will have to look beyond their role and take a buyer-centered perspective. Are there new sources of revenue? Is there a way to make a costly situation profitable? Is there a different financial model that could be applied and thereby accrue financial benefits?

7. **Build a Solution Road Map.** Sellers must be able to make change low risk for the buying organization. Every seller must be an implementation specialist. They should know the fears that underlie a purchasing decision and offer a road map that is, to a large measure, risk free.

Every executive conversation should serve as a platform for developing steps a seller can take to provide meaningful value for the executive.

## Executive Readiness Guide

The Executive Readiness Guide shown at the end of this chapter in Addendum 11, is designed to help sellers prepare for executive conversations by testing industry and business knowledge, familiarity with corporate initiatives, and tactical plans for the conversation itself.

## Key Points to Remember for Buyer-Centered Sellers

1. The challenge facing the seller is to determine who from the buying organization can make an impact on the buying process or decision, when contact would be most beneficial, and how an executive would benefit from a meeting with the seller.

2. It is always best to sell to the executive who owns the problem, opportunity, or threat. In some cases, this will mean selling to a supervisor, manager, or director while in others it will mean selling to the leadership team.

3. Sellers should conduct a thoughtful review before they initiate an executive level conversation.

4. There are four factors that may justify an executive conversation. They are the "Tipping Points."

5. Sellers should carefully research their Executive Buyer and be prepared for the questions they will most likely receive during the meeting.

6. Sellers should be prepared to answer the seven tough conversation stopping questions or comments.

7. Sellers can build their credibility in seven different ways: uncover hidden problems, identify key resources, build internal consensus, quantify and document value, identify key costs and risks, capture an opportunity or competitive advantage, and build a solution road map.

## THE SKILL CHALLENGE

In order to become more effective and buyer centered, what skill can you identify from the content in this chapter that requires skill and practice? Please write it here or on a separate sheet of paper.

_____

_____

_____

_____

_____

_____

_____

_____

_____

_____

_____

_____

_____

_____

## ADDENDUM 11: EXECUTIVE READINESS GUIDE

Sellers who want to improve their executive selling skills can use this Executive Readiness Guide to prepare for executive conversations.

### PRE-CALL QUESTIONS

#### Industry and Business Knowledge
- ☐ What trends characterize your customer's industry?
- ☐ What primary market forces are at play, and how will this affect your customer's business model?
- ☐ How are your customer's competitors responding to market forces?
- ☐ What do industry experts forecast for their industry's next 18 months?
- ☐ What financial hurdles is your customer facing?
- ☐ What near-term threats and opportunities is your customer facing?

#### Corporate Initiatives/Needs/Benefits
- ☐ Is your customer pursuing new sources of revenue?
- ☐ What are your customer's most urgent initiatives?
- ☐ How will you explore your customer's priorities?
- ☐ How does your customer measure success?
- ☐ How do they measure return, benefits, and value?
- ☐ What initiatives are draining resources, time, and dollars?
- ☐ How will you document value, and how does that metric align with your customer's dashboard?

#### Buyer-Centered Conversation Skills
- ☐ Have you developed and rehearsed your sales call plan?
- ☐ What questions will you ask to determine the problem, opportunity or threat your client is facing?
- ☐ How would you determine the current state, future state and gap to show the cost of inaction?

☐ What "foundation" questions will you use to explore the client's challenges and the status of their initiatives?

☐ How will you uncover your client's priorities and determine the scope and immediacy for action?

☐ How will you secure an advance from your client to promote future discussion?

☐ What is your solution, and what does it do for your customer?

☐ How does this conversation align with the buying process?

## POST-CALL REVIEW: INDUSTRY AND BUSINESS KNOWLEDGE

☐ How did you demonstrate industry knowledge?

☐ What did you learn about your customer's view of market forces?

☐ What did you learn about their view of their competitive landscape?

☐ What threats to your customer surfaced in the conversation?

### Corporate Initiatives/Needs/Concerns

☐ What organizational needs or concerns are they attempting to address with the purchase of your product?

☐ Were you able to draw a link between your product and the customer's organizational needs?

☐ Did you uncover any changes or surprises in their financial focus?

☐ Did you learn anything that clarifies how they make decisions?

☐ What does your competitive landscape look like? Any surprises?

☐ What's the level of urgency?

☐ What have they purchased recently? What financial measures were critical to that buying decision?

☐ How does your sales opportunity support or compete with high-ranking initiatives?

## Buyer-Centered Conversation Skills

☐ What went well and seemed to resonate with your client?

☐ Do you better understand your client's challenges, priorities, and sense of urgency?

☐ What went poorly and seemed to bore, annoy, or confuse your customer?

☐ How will this conversation change the buying process for this decision?

☐ Are any modifications to your value message necessary?

☐ What terminology did your customer use to discuss value or identify key performance indicators?

# Chapter 10

# Is Your Cross-Selling Program Driving You Crazy?

"Don't find customers for your products—find products for your customers."

Seth Godin—Author of 18 Bestsellers

In many industries, consolidation of competitors has made cross-selling a logical strategy for driving organic growth and improving sales productivity. Within organizations, companies have implemented cross-selling efforts to introduce new products and expand their footprint within an existing customer base.

From the executive suite, the development and implementation of a cross-selling program can seem like an easy call. It's supposed to be an automatic "game changer." You sell more and faster, exceed quotas, and capture additional market share. The customers who have loved you in the past will welcome you with open wallets. Right?

Well, maybe not! While many cross-selling programs are effective, many more create confusion that lowers productivity, disappoints customers, and compromises margins. If not planned properly, cross-selling can erode trust and credibility.

If you find yourself on the implementation end of someone else's game plan, take a deep breath, relax, and get a firm grip on cross-selling, the barriers to selling, and the best practices for developing a buyer-centered approach that will guide your sales activity. If you think you are alone, consider this story of cross-selling.

### Story: Cross-Selling Gone Very Wrong

A couple of years ago, we were working with a company in the medical device industry that had acquired two smaller device manufacturers. Nothing new or unusual about that; it is all part of ongoing consolidation in the healthcare sector. The troublesome part was their efforts at building an integrated cross-selling plan. They were having difficulty answering a simple question: "Who is going to sell what to whom and how?" In other words, "How will we leverage the entirety of our sales and marketing resources to cross-sell all three portfolios?"

From an executive perspective, they had all the pieces neatly in place. They had formed a steering committee with executives from the three organizations. The marketing team crafted attractive and informative brochures, and updated the website and the training materials. Sales targets had been identified. Adjustments had been made in the commission program to incentivize cross-selling. All the elements were positioned for a rollout. Well...not everything. Many questions remained.

When we visited with sales representatives, the process became less clear. Representatives from the parent company felt that their product portfolio should be the "lead" product in any selling process. Representatives from the acquired companies thought their traditional products should lead, and the parent company's product should "follow." Everyone agreed on one principle: sell your portfolio first, and sell from another portfolio only when or if there is a clear and unobstructed pathway to a purchasing decision.

When we spoke with sales managers, other concerns surfaced. Not all products in a portfolio are equal. Some products drive revenue but have lower margins, while others have higher margins but generate lower revenue. Further, some products have a longer sales cycle and require more extensive resources (presentations, product testing, etc.).

Some sellers weren't comfortable selling a different product. With some, it was lack of interest. With others, it was a reluctance to learn the technology. With others, it would take more time.

"Which product should lead in the selling process?" "Should high margin products warrant the most attention?" "How should managers bring all representatives up to speed on all products?" "Have we chosen the right customers?" "Is the commission plan fair?"

---

## The Challenge of Buyer-Centered Selling

*The Buyer's Dilemma:* **Many stakeholders, buying committees and groups are faced with tough choices among suppliers who provide a portfolio of products to different departments, divisions, and geographical markets.** Should we trust sole sourcing of critical supplies? Should we encourage competition among suppliers? What are the risks? What are the benefits?

*The Seller's Challenge:* **Selling new products to existing customers can be a challenging task that requires a fresh look at who, why, and how your customer buys.** Buyer-centered sellers strive to understand the political, personal, and financial issues underlying how buyers view them, their company, and their product/service.

---

Today's sellers are faced with cross-selling programs that have aggressive financial quotas but little guidance on how to qualify and engage prospects. Cross-selling may appear deceptively simple. Matching the right buyer with the right product can be quite a complex matter.

In this chapter, we explore the issues surrounding cross-selling, why cross-selling programs fail, and how top performers seem to miraculously win when challenged by surprises and ambiguities.

## WHAT IS CROSS-SELLING?

This should be an easy question, but the variety of answers is part of the problem. Different disciplines (such as retail sales) have different definitions and describe the process of cross-selling in different ways. Retail marketers use the merchandising of related products to cross-sell. For example, clothing stores display a suit with other "related" products—ties, shirts, belts, and shoes. Order takers in fast food restaurants may ask the buyer, "Would you like an order of chicken nuggets to accompany your burger?" Cashiers in some grocery stores will ask if you need stamps or ice. These are hardly the same selling processes, and neither captures the model of cross-selling we are addressing in this chapter.

> Cross-selling is the process of leveraging existing positive relationships and business intelligence to sell an additional product or service to an existing customer."

We are defining cross-selling as: "the process of leveraging existing positive relationships and business intelligence to sell an additional product or service to an existing customer."

As you can imagine, deciding what is or isn't cross-selling entails many complexities. Here are four issues and how they apply to our discussion.

- **Must the selling process be direct?** For this chapter, we are limiting cross-selling to the direct selling processes. Other business disciplines may take a different approach.

- **Must the selling occur across product categories?** The origin of the phrase "cross-selling" comes from the intent to sell across product categories. However, the rules can change greatly from one business to another. The answer is: no, not necessarily.

- **Must cross-selling target existing customers?** Many executives point to the leveraging of existing customers as a defining characteristic of cross-selling. But does that mean the same buyers? The same department but different buyers? Or, the same organization but different buyers? Without a common understanding of the target, both sellers and buyers get caught in a cycle of confusion. Cross-selling programs include all these variations as well as conducting research, interacting with new stakeholders, etc.

- **Must cross-selling involve the same buying process as other products?** Some argue that unless the seller is selling to a common buying team and process, cross-selling makes little or no sense. Why focus on cross-selling if you can't benefit from a history of understanding the company and how it chooses to buy? As the buying processes in many organizations have increased in complexity, sellers continue to find themselves facing different buyers, stakeholders, and influencers, even within the same department or silo. New and different buyers can offer the seller an opportunity or a significant challenge.

To our frontline sellers, these issues are personal. They complicate each seller's investment of time and compromise their productivity. Management would do well to listen to the men and women on the front lines.

This is what we often hear from sales representatives and account managers charged with rolling out a new cross-selling program in a B2B environment.

- *"Nobody knows who owns this account."*
- *"There is no clear direction on how to coordinate selling processes between ourselves and the other teams."*
- *"My colleagues won't listen to me about how to approach this customer."*
- *"My customers are fed up with twice as many sales representatives calling for appointments."*
- *"My customer said she isn't interested in this product. Now what do I do?"*
- *"My customers are confused about who they should call for service. How can we get back to one-stop service?"*
- *"We're getting lots of introductions and meetings…but no new sales."*

The reality of cross-selling in the retail arena is success after success. Amazon estimates that approximately 35% of its sales are attributable to cross-selling.[1] In B2B sales, cross-selling has a bit of a checkered past. Let's look at why cross-selling programs fail.

## WHY DO CROSS-SELLING PROGRAMS FAIL?

When cross-selling programs fail, there is ample blame to cover sales managers and frontline sellers. Let's take a close look at four roadblocks that some sellers and sales managers fail to heed.

1. **Poor Match of Products and Customers.** Imagine the following scenario. Your portfolio includes seven or eight devices that are vital to complex surgical procedures. These products are real revenue generators. You have developed strong value messages to support the selling process, and the clinical teams continue to endorse and use your products. While Procurement is involved in the buying process, they have purchased the products at or near market price. But now you are faced with cross-selling several products that are viewed as less essential by the buying organization. Procurement buys these items in bulk and at heavily discounted prices.

   Several problems may arise. First, your organization might be viewed differently by the buying organization. Instead of being a trusted provider of essential clinical products, buyers may view you as a provider of bulk commodities. Second, the discounting that buyers expect for your non-essential products may be extended to your revenue generating surgical devices. Some executive in Procurement may think, "If they have built a discount into their price strategy for their non-essentials, perhaps we can get a similar discount on their high-priced surgical devices."

   Last, you may find your organization (and your cross-selling teams) traversing a different competitive landscape. This may require careful updates and revisions to your sales playbooks.

**Recommended Action:** Be careful with your product mix. You don't have to cross-sell all products in all portfolios. Debrief with customers, and solicit feedback. Determine where an opportunity may exist.

2. **Poor Understanding of Why Customers Cross-Buy.** There is no question that cross-selling may benefit the selling organization. But why would a customer want to buy a broader portfolio of products from one company? Buyer-centered sellers are careful to evaluate the process from the customer's perspective. Consider all the downside issues of a sole-source or limited-source supplier. There must be substantial trust in the supplier to provide quality products on time and at a competitive price. Not all buyers want to put all their eggs in one basket. They may be reluctant to give a seller more volume.

   **Recommended Action:** Develop a sales playbook (for each product) that identifies the buyer's "persona," the problems the products solve, competitors, and anticipated concerns, along with tactics for neutralizing the concerns. Above all, mitigate the buyer's risk of buying from a single supplier. This requires business acumen, research, discovery, and hard work.

3. **Failure to Identify Who Is Likely to Cross-Buy.** Many cross-sell programs fail to identify in advance a profile of the ideal cross-sell target. Who is more likely to buy? Are we more likely to succeed by selling to a customer who has participated in other decisions that resulted in a purchase of our products? What are the demographic, behavioral, organizational, and psychographic characteristics of a favorable buyer?

   **Recommended Action:** Develop an "ideal cross-buy customer profile," and apply this profile or scorecard to qualify and prioritize each prospect.

4. **Selection of Poor Customers.** The notion that "any customer is a good customer" can quickly undermine a company's cross-selling

plan. In a *Harvard Business Review* article, Shah and Kumar identify four characteristics of cross-buyers that make them poor prospects.[2]

    a. The "service demanders" are the cross-buyers who are willing to buy the product(s) but demand the delivery of additional services and resources.

    b. The "revenue reversers" may cross-buy only to return products, thereby erasing revenue and profits.

    c. The "promotion maximizers" are drawn to steep discounts that erode profits.

    d. "Spending limiters" have limited spending power because of tightening budgets or a supplier management practice. Spending too much time and resources on poor customers can derail your cross-selling plan.

**Recommended Action:** Know your prospects, their buying motives, and their tendencies. Identify and avoid customers with buying practices that consume resources, minimize profits, or restrict purchasing.

Sales management (including regional managers, customer service managers, sales operations and division vice presidents) must shoulder much of the responsibility for failed or stalled cross-selling programs. In their rush to launch and capture ambitious program revenue goals, sales managers are guilty of these five shortcomings.

1. **The Shotgun Start.** We have this terrible image in mind of a domestic sales team standing abreast at a starting line, poised for the sales vice president to launch a cross-sell program by firing a starter's gun. All too many companies begin their cross-sell program with the blare of a trumpet and a timed domestic launch. There is no pilot effort or beta test prior to a shotgun start. This usually signals:

   • Poor planning.
   • No sales skill training to address differences in the buy-sell process.

- No team coordination prior to launch.
- No feedback from the field.

**Recommended Action:** Conduct a pilot project with experienced sellers in a well-developed market. Choose your target customers carefully. Collect data and debrief with frontline sellers. Identify best practices and appropriate program metrics.

2. **No Cross-Training—Just Cross-Selling.** All too often, companies assume that if their sales representatives and manager are skilled in selling one product, their skills and knowledge will be transferable to a larger, more diversified portfolio of products. This may not be the case. Not every sales representative is capable of learning to sell the new products, and some may not have the desire.

   **Recommended Action:** Product knowledge is table stakes to effectively cross-sell. Develop and implement a sales training program prior to launch. This program should focus on understanding the buyer and their Problems, Opportunities, and Threats (POT). Sellers should be provided with "insights" and the questions to ask a buyer to uncover a POT. The goal of the training is to arm the seller with the ammunition to get the buyer out of status quo by getting them to see the difference between their current state and a better future state.

   Update and reinforce sales skills through peer-to-peer in-process training. Use sales directors and field representatives to aid in coaching the frontline team. Use video-taped role playing and other methods to measure competency. Practice should occur with peers and managers and not in front of the customer.

3. **Not Communicating with the Field.** Too often sales executives are quick to share news of a win or celebrate quarterly quota achievements, but they overlook the selling practices that helped achieve the win. During any cross-sell program, sellers and account managers can provide optics into best practices. What information does a cross-buyer

want? What value messages resonate for specific products? Every win should shed light on selling practices that positively impact customers.

**Recommended Action:** Conduct rigorous "what worked-what didn't" analyses that identify best and unsuccessful practices. Aggregate the best practices, and share them with field sales representatives. Above all, talk to the customers. Learn what they liked and disliked.

4. **Failure to measure success and progress.** Almost every sales manager measures program success with a quantitative yardstick. How many cross-sells did we achieve this quarter? What's the impact on revenue? However, few sales managers measure qualitative progress. Success answers the question, "Are we getting the results we want?" Progress tells us if we are getting the desired results for the right reasons. "Have we implemented and executed the tactics necessary to replicate and advance our success?"

   **Recommended Action:** When developing your dashboard for evaluating a team's cross-selling efforts, combine outcome measures or lagging indicators (revenue, product volume, share of wallet) with behavioral indices or leading indicators (access to new stakeholders, executive support).

5. **Conflicting or Misunderstood Incentives.** Do field representatives fully understand the incentives and how they apply to the cross-selling program? Often, we have reviewed commission plans that were intended to promote cross-selling, but they did little to promote program goals, or they were open to misinterpretation. For example, one commission program dramatically increased the commissions payable on cross-sold products, but the definition of which products could be counted as cross-sold products was so loose, sellers loaded up their customers with unnecessary products that were later returned for credit. In another situation, the commissions were variable among different products. Guess what happened? The sales force cross-sold only the products with the highest commission.

**Recommended Action**: Solicit feedback from your high producing sellers about the commission program. Have as many sets of eyes as possible review your plan prior to launch. Structure the commission program to encourage cross-selling of all products in the program.

## HOW DO BUYER-CENTERED SELLERS WIN AT CROSS-SELLING?

Buyer-centered sellers report the following keys as essential to their success.

Figure 10-1: How Buyer-Centered Sellers Win at Cross Selling

1. **Work & Sell Collaboratively.** Cross-selling often involves coordinating sellers with overlapping portfolios in the same region. Winning sellers are seldom "loners." They coordinate their sales strategy and economize their efforts by planning with their teammates. They share insight on buyer purchasing habits, customer priorities, and best practices.

   **Recommended Action**: Identify "team selling" opportunities and accounts that have dual ownership or require a mix of sellers and technical specialists to optimize the cross-selling opportunities. Buyer-centered sellers often formalize communication with team members and establish responsibilities and timelines.

- Settle issues of account ownership early.
- Target and qualify opportunities together.
- Jointly determine priorities, time frames, and selling responsibilities.
- Establish periodic meetings or calls to review the status of each cross-selling opportunity. It's far better to win as a team than to find yourself alone, outflanked, outnumbered, and outsold.

2. **Understand Fully Each Buyer's Perspective.** Prior to the launch of cross-selling efforts for an account, steps should be taken to understand the buyer's perspective. There is no rule that says: "Thou shall cross-sell to all customers." Qualify and target only those customers who have needs that align well with your portfolio of new products and services and that can provide the customer outcomes required.

**Recommended Action:**
- Explore the buyer's underlying needs, and determine possible connections between the expanded portfolio of products and the buying organization's key initiatives.[3]
- Determine how essential the products are to all buyers. Remember that sellers don't have to cross-sell all products in their expanded portfolio.
- Verify that your customer is satisfied with their existing customer experience before you attempt to cross sell.
- Survey to what degree cross-buying would appeal to the buying organization. Are there cultural or procedural restrictions on buying additional products from a single supplier?
- Determine which of your customers are firmly entrenched with a competitor's product.
- Determine whether the buyer perceives any risk from increasing their spend with your company.

3. **Sell the "Right" Products to the "Right" Customer.** Not all products are attractive to all customers. This means understanding what

your product means for your customer. Is it essential? Is the need urgent? Are they under contract with a competitor? Are they loyal to a specific supplier?

Figure 10-2: Cross-Sell Decision Map

In many regards, it's vital to build an ideal opportunity profile by building a cross-sell decision map that carefully qualifies all cross-sell prospects against current profile criteria. Combine training, planning, and periodic feedback into a pilot cross-sell program. Measure both success and execution. Set clear expectations, and recognize and reward achievement.

**Recommended Action:** In the Cross-Sell Decision Map, there are two primary factors in making a cross-sell decision: type of customer (poor or excellent) and how essential your product or service is to the buyer.

The type of customer is subjective but might include factors such as openness to change, type of relationship desired, payment history, buying process, etc. with each factor weighted.

An essential product is defined as one that a buyer must have available to serve their customer base.

- If the customer is a "poor" one and your product is viewed as non-essential, you may want to reconsider this sales opportunity. It offers minimal chance for success, and the customer is likely to make decisions based on price. They will require a lot of attention and service resources.

- If the customer is "poor" and the product is essential, this is a potential cross-sell opportunity. The customer may be receptive to your product or service, but because they are designated as a poor customer, the seller should proceed with caution. Poor customers tend to stay poor customers, just with increased business volume.

- If the customer is "excellent" but your product is non-essential, this is an above average opportunity because you have a strong working relationship. To cross-sell products, it's imperative that sellers leverage their business relationship and proven value. As an example, a bundling price strategy might be an effective way to gain additional business and keep competitors out.

- The last option is your best bet: an excellent customer who believes your product is essential. This is an ideal opportunity. Whenever you find this combination of factors, swing for the fences.

4. **Understand Differences in the Buying Processes.** It's easy to assume that two buyers from the same organization are likely to undertake the same or similar buying processes. That could be a big mistake. Research confirms that companies are turning to large buying teams with complex review and decision-making processes. Conduct your reconnaissance early, and choose wisely.

**Recommended Action:**
- Check with internal resources to gain an overview of the buying process and "buyer's window."
- Answer this question: "Do you have the time, resources, and skill set to compete against the current supplier?"
- Identify the membership of the buying team, and determine whether the composition of the group provides you enough support.

5. **Understand the Broader Competitive Landscape.** Whenever a company embarks on a cross-selling program, sellers may find themselves facing different or unanticipated competition. While sellers may be well entrenched as a preferred supplier of one product, a competitor may be equally connected for a second product.

**Recommended Action:**
- Update sales playbooks to identify new competitive forces and appropriate product positioning.
- Track where competitors succeed and fail.
- Evaluate each competitor's internal support or adversaries.

Many top performers rely on a "White Space Worksheet" to identify and prioritize sales targets within an account. As illustrated in Figure 10-3, "white space" is a reference to any sales opportunity between a customer and one of your products.

It's easy to build a White Space Worksheet. On the horizontal axis, list the names of the existing products that you sell. On the vertical axis, list each current customer. Then place an "X" in the appropriate box to show which products have been purchased from your firm in the last year (see Figure 10-3 by customer). This is the book of business you want to protect so that you receive the repeat business.

| Customer | Product A | Product B | Product C | Product D |
|----------|-----------|-----------|-----------|-----------|
| A | X | | | |
| B | | X | | |
| C | | | X | |
| D | | | | X |
| E | X | | | |
| F | | X | | |
| G | | | X | |

Figure 10-3: Visual of Existing Products Sold to Existing Customers

Now add a "Y" to your Worksheet where every customer is buying one of your cross-selling products or services from a competitor or has developed their own internal solution. If the customer has a contract in place with a competitor that will preclude you from cross-selling to them this year, insert a "Y-1" if it's a one-year contract or a "Y-2" if it's a two-year contract, etc. (See Figure 10-4).

| Customer | Product A | Product B | Product C | Product D |
|----------|-----------|-----------|-----------|-----------|
| A | X | Y | Y | Y |
| B | Y | X | Y-1 | Y |
| C | Y | Y | X | Y |
| D | Y | Y | Y | X |
| E | X | Y | Y | Y |
| F | Y | X | Y | Y |
| G | Y | Y | X | Y-2 |

Figure 10-4: Visual of Products Purchased by Customers

The Ys are your Opportunity and your immediate target for cross-selling. The "Y" is for conversion to your product immediately, and the "Y-1 or 2" is a target when the contract is open for renegotiation. This doesn't mean you shouldn't spend time cultivating this business until it's up for renewal, but it does mean that your selling activity for that product with that account will not provide you revenue this year or next unless the current contract can be cancelled or your company can be added as a secondary supplier.

The next step is for sellers to prioritize the sales potential by customer-by product (see Figure 10-5).

| Customer | Product A | Product B | Product C | Product D |
|----------|-----------|-----------|-----------|-----------|
| A | X | $80K | $64K | $100K |
| B | $240K | X | Y-1 | $125K |
| C | $260K | $93K | X | $75K |
| D | $350K | $220K | $175K | X |
| E | X | $140K | $200K | $90K |
| F | $300K | X | $150K | $50K |
| G | $173K | $117K | X | Y-1 |

Figure 10-5: Our Sales Potential for Cross-Selling

Taking the few minutes to conduct this analysis provides the seller with a clear focus of where to spend their time most effectively.

### Final Thoughts for Sellers

Don't get obsessed with the sale—focus on developing the account. Develop relationships high, wide, and deep based on the value you bring through insights and helping them see a problem, opportunity, or threat that was unrecognized. Expand your champions and advocates. Connect the senior team of your organization with the senior team of the buying organization. You'll be surprised at how quickly sales come to you instead of you chasing them.

Your greatest asset is your knowledge of the buying organization's priorities and initiatives. Daily, ask yourself, "How can we (through our broad portfolio of products and services) help our customers achieve their goals?" Cross-selling is less about selling than developing a vital, sustainable partnership that helps your customers achieve their business goals.

## Final Thoughts for Sales Managers

Too many companies justify internally their cross-selling programs as a "strategic approach to selling more product (or services) to existing customers." That may be well and good, but it doesn't say much about the company's commitment to their customers. Consider an alternative justification that may well attract and interest your customers: As we uncover unrecognized and unmet customer needs, we are better positioned than ever to help our best customers solve problems and satisfy needs. Put the rationale for cross-selling on helping the customer, not on selling additional products. Make the rationale buyer centered.

Cross-selling is more than a change in focus—it's a change in culture for the sales organization. The greatest risk lies in disappointing existing customers by failing to deliver on a product that is unfamiliar to the seller and vital to a buyer. While many sellers are loners, cross-selling is most effective when teams of sellers share their product and customer knowledge.

## Key Points to Remember for Buyer-Centered Sellers

1. Be careful when matching products to prospects; you don't need to sell all your products to every buyer.
2. Develop a scorecard to aid in prioritizing cross-selling opportunities.
3. Selecting poor customers can undermine your cross-selling efforts.
4. Identify essential resources early, and work together as a selling team to win the sale.
5. A Cross-Sell Decision Map can help you determine how buyers will perceive your products.
6. There may be significant differences in the buying process from year to year, department to department, and product to product.
7. A White Space Worksheet can help you identify and prioritize cross-sell opportunities.

## THE SKILL CHALLENGE

In order to become more effective and buyer centered, what skill can you identify from the content in this chapter that requires skill and practice? Please write it here or on a separate sheet of paper.

_____

_____

_____

_____

_____

_____

_____

_____

_____

_____

_____

_____

_____

_____

_____

# Chapter 11

# Secrets of Closing Like a Pro

"Making money is a wonderful side effect of closing well. But life is about more than making money; it's about making a difference in the lives of others."

James Muir—Author of *The Perfect Close*

One factor common to all sales professionals is the nagging suspicion and doubt that surfaces in our thoughts as we approach the finalization of a major deal. Have I answered all my customer's questions? Will they attempt to drive down my price? Can I count on everyone's support, or have I overlooked someone who could derail the close by introducing unforeseen challenges? What could my competitor do to upset the deal?

We are discovering that, even with meticulous attention to the beginning of a sale, we have no idea how each story will end. Traditionally, salespeople have left the close of a deal to happenstance, without a plan or architecture that could resolve each deal in a way that benefits both sides.

*The Perfect Close,* author, James Muir, highlights a scary finding uncovered from Neil Rackham's research. Muir writes, "Professionals sell about half of what they set out to sell. For a decade or more, quota attainment by professional sales reps has hovered between 50% and 60%, and most recently, quota attainment has been trending downward."[1] That's a pretty strong wake-up call for most of us. Further, Muir reports a finding that sets off more alarms. Typical closing techniques appear to undermine a seller's sales success. The greater the percentage of traditional closing behavior, the lower the success rate.[2]

## Story: Details Matter

Stacey worked for a global beverage company and was about to finalize a deal with a national restaurant chain. The deal would involve taking the business away from her biggest competitor and would provide an incredible commission for her and a boost to her career. Stacey believed she was well positioned with the Executive Buyer and other stakeholders but still had this nagging feeling that she was missing something. She looked over her most recent email from the buyer. Nothing seemed unusual except for one small point. He was changing the meeting location. Then the bell went off for Stacey. He was changing the meeting to a room at the buyer's corporate offices. Uh, oh! Could this mean that the buyer is accommodating someone's schedule from the executive leadership team? "I better give him a call and see if anyone else will be participating." Good move on Stacey's part. A senior vice president wanted to "talk through some issues" and would be attending the session. Stacey placed a call to her boss and obtained his commitment to attend the meeting as well. It was a vital move for Stacey's success. Her boss encouraged her to reach out to the buyer's senior vice president, offer to share how her product would deliver value to her customer, and answer key questions ahead of time. The vice president's comment at the end of the phone conversation was telling. "I just wanted to protect our interests in a deal of this size, and it sounds like you and our team have thought through the value questions that have been on my mind, especially with the big-ticket issues. You've just saved me a couple of hours on my schedule. I look forward to working with you in the future, Stacy." Always nice to be alert, anticipate your challenges, and bring in "backup" when you most need it.

Many deal closings are burdened by a variety of complexities, including the challenge of eliciting and negotiating commitments and managing unexpected issues that may surface at the last moment. Managing these details often requires the conflict management skills of a psychiatrist, the planning and calculations of a financial planner, and the calm of a diplomat.

---

## The Challenge of Buyer-Centered Selling

***The Buyer's Dilemma:* Buyers often face fears and concerns before closing an important and complex deal. If left unaddressed, these concerns may explode into paralyzing or deal-killing emotions.** Executive Buyers often experience "buyer's remorse" and begin second-guessing their decision. "Have I gotten what I need?" "How will others view my decision?" "Is everyone supportive of the decision?"

***The Seller's Challenge:* Every seller is faced with the task of blending the buyer's needs and expectations with commitments that unify the buyer and seller.** No deal is guaranteed until it closes. The most acute threat to closure can be fear spawned by unaddressed risks. As sellers move toward finalizing a complex B2B sale, many overlook the strategy that brought them to this point. Instead of moving closer to a unified agreement, they often begin to see each other as adversaries. Suddenly, the deal that seemed so clear-cut and secure begins to fall apart.

---

The answer? Prepare! Continue to differentiate your solution. Gain commitment from the buyer. Share value that motivates your prospect to buy. Be alert, follow up on unusual details, and anticipate the unexpected even if it arises after you have covered all your bases. Do your homework, and close like a pro.

## WHAT DOES IT MEAN TO "CLOSE" A DEAL?

The term "close" is often misunderstood and misleading. Closure is a process of blending the buyer's and seller's expectations into mutually beneficial commitments that are binding. It is not an event, phone call, handshake, requisition, or purchase order—although each can contribute to a close. It is the forging of common business expectations and commitments into an accord that serves both parties. "If you do X, then I will do Y."

> Closure is a process of blending the buyer's and seller's expectations into mutually beneficial commitments that are binding.

Many sellers assume the close will be a few minutes, hours, or days at the end of the buy-sell process. It will be the "wrap-up," the "contract," the "purchase order", "the irrevocable letter of credit" or the "consulting or purchased services agreement". If, at the end of an extended buy-sell process, all the seller has achieved is a legal document, then the seller has wasted the opportunity to forge something greater: a business partnership born of value and driven by mutual commitments throughout the buyer's journey.

Unfortunately, all closes are not the same. Even within the same market, some sellers conclude deals with simple closes, while their colleagues are faced with complex closes that require hours of discussion and negotiation. A simple close is an agreement that has three characteristics:

- One-on-one selling and negotiation
- Sale of a single product
- Clear expectations about what buyer and seller wish to gain from the deal

But some sales opportunities that begin as simple deals can quickly morph into more difficult, multi-faceted, and time intensive agreements. How? The buying organization may be undergoing changes that complicate the deal and pose barriers to closure. To name a few obstacles, the buyer may want:

- Non-traditional payment provisions
- Delivery provisions that are costly to the seller

- Greater or fewer products in future years
- Customized packaging

Suddenly, a simple close turns into a complex one.

In some cases, negotiating the close of a deal can be more challenging than the selling process. Complex closes may require the planning of an architect, while simple closes can be served by a phone call or the exchange of emails. Multiple buyers, a challenging menu of products, pricing options, and a buyer's confusion about the needs of the buying organization can complicate the buying process and the close.

## HARSH REALITIES OF CLOSING THE SALE

There are several realities that may be disturbing to many sellers and can account for declining close ratios across industries.[3]

1. **Deferring the close to the end of the buying process may raise "red flags."** The buyer may think, "What am I getting myself into?" "If I agree to this deal, what are the unseen implications?" This causes the buyer to worry about agreeing to commitments that are unclear.

   **Recommended Action.** Buyer-centered sellers check their buyer's sensitivity to risk and concern for unseen threats. In Miller and Heiman's *Conceptual Selling,* they refer to a "basic issue" as a potential threat that has remained unspoken but could jeopardize the deal.[4] If you suspect the buyer is harboring an unaddressed issue, don't leave the meeting or conclude a phone call without addressing the buyer's concerns.

2. **Some closing techniques are toxic.** By toxic, we mean aggressive or manipulative. A "gentle nudge" by the seller may appear to be the equivalent of a head-on car wreck. Any tactic that prompts a defensive or competitive response may be a serious error in your closing strategy. Make no mistake, buyers know what you are doing and may not appreciate the push-and-shove technique.

   **Recommended Action.** Questions play a vital role in setting the tone and temper of a close. Buyer-centered sellers ask questions to re-engage the buyer and open their eyes to options while appearing flexible. "We've covered a lot of ground in a short period of time. How comfortable are you with what we've put together for our companies? Is there a single provision that we should revisit?"

3.  **Sales don't close well when left to close by accident.** That's like getting the car up to speed, heading in the right direction, and then taking your hands off the steering wheel. It's unlikely that the deal will automatically head in the direction you desire. You may be very comfortable with the process, but how does your buyer feel? Have you and your buyer been completely transparent with each other?

    **Recommended Action:** Give thought to using "advances" or small mutual agreements that will drive the buying process forward. Make sure your value messaging creates a sense of urgency. If there is no compelling reason for the buyer to make a change now, don't expect change to happen immediately.

4.  **Rapport doesn't beat trust.** It's easy to assume that, because you've built a strong rapport with someone, they trust you. That may overstate your position. Your customer may like you and enjoy your company without trusting you, your solution, or your organization. Rapport allows you access, but it says little about your overall capability, the performance of your solution, or the veracity of your pledge to deliver value. Trust, not rapport, is critical for driving a negotiated settlement.

    At the heart of trust is credibility. "Can we trust that your solution will deliver the desired results?" "Can we count on your company providing the resources promised and agreed upon in our negotiated agreement?"

    **Recommended Action.** Evaluate whether you have built rapport alone or if you have also developed the credibility necessary to engender trust by testing your customer's willingness to act. In every stage of the buyer's journey, buyer-centered sellers question their customers on priorities and needs. Transparency is therapeutic for both parties.

Think in terms of reinforcing your credibility at every step. Share the results from similar sales. Remind your customer of your business case and the ROI. Be willing to address service issues and response time. Don't focus on the worst-case scenario, but be willing to add precautionary measures as needed.

## WHAT IS THE "ARCHITECTURE OF A CLOSE?"

When a builder purchases a plot of land, there are strategic questions that require an answer. What services am I intending to provide? How can I maximize revenue when compared to my costs? What is my timeframe? What expectations will potential consumers or customers have for my use of the land?

### Core Elements of a Close

On a much smaller scale, similar questions and answers are necessary to build a foundation and guide a deal to closure. Consider these five core elements when closing a deal.

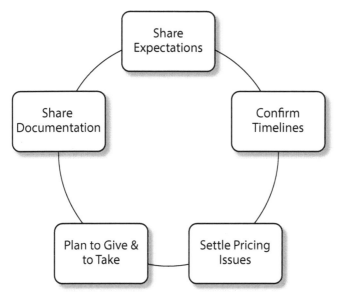

Figure 11-1: Five Core Elements of a Close

1. **Share Expectations.** During the buying process, the seller discovers expectations held by the buyer. These expectations may become the focus of sales calls, conversations, and emails as buyers and sellers attempt to clarify each other's needs and test one another's flexibility. Ultimately, these expectations may set the agenda for discussions that lead to a finalized agreement. Buyer-centered sellers plan conversations that reveal problems, opportunities, threats, options, priorities, and risks. The seller must "own" the close and bring the buyer into agreement on what key issues should be discussed. Both buyer and seller create and manage an agenda that defines the order that key issues will be discussed.

2. **Confirm Timelines.** Deadlines can become thorny issues, especially when buyers are changing suppliers. Complications with timelines are two-fold: timelines often change over the course of the buying process, and an Executive Buyer may not be aware of all the timeframes until late in the discussions. The seller should always seek to confirm the "buyer's window." When is the buying organization expecting the deal to reach finality? Savvy sellers ask the buyer, "On what date would you like to be operational with our solution so you can begin to accrue the ROI we discussed?" Sometimes buyers and sellers use imaginary or exaggerated timelines to create pressure on their counterpart. It's an unhealthy and trust-destroying tactic for buyer and seller.

3. **Settle Pricing Issues.** In many industries, demands for seller discounts or favorable payment conditions are a normal course of business and an essential element in every finalized agreement. Buyer-centered sellers conduct price discussions throughout the buying process. They want to avoid the chance for the buyer to suffer sticker shock and lay a foundation for value that supports a higher price point.

4. **Plan to Give & to Take.** Prior to finalizing a complex deal, buyer-centered sellers plot their "give and take" exchange. Professional negotiators refer to these exchanges as part of a concession plan. Concession

plans answer basic questions that, if unanticipated, can result in the loss of revenue. Concessions can take several forms. A buyer can ask for a concession (let's say a 5% discount in price), and the seller may decide that the amount is too small to argue about and literally may give away the 5% in order to finalize the deal quickly. A second type of concession is the authorization of a portion of the 5% discount (let's say 3%) and the offer of the perceived balance of the provision in a non-monetary concession (more frequent product delivery). In either case, the seller should frame a reciprocal request—what the seller wishes to receive in return. All sellers should prepare a plan of "trades" and "bundles" as forms of give-and-take. If the buyer wants something, what can you ask for in return?

5. **Share Documentation.** As the deal is finalized, there has to be some document that describes agreed upon terms, conditions, and provisions. Top performers "own" formal records of the close. Share the mutual commitments of the close by email, letter of agreement, and contract.

## Fueling the Close Process

In *The Perfect Close,* James Muir identifies the process required to fuel closing, and it doesn't involve pushing a bunch of levers that apply pressure on the buyer. Muir is quick to warn that pressure techniques can have a negative effect on decision-making. The primary fuel for moving the buying process forward is a steady dose of value messaging.[5] By conveying value, sellers energize their buyer. The buyer is more likely to act in a way that drives the buying process forward.

## Story: The Tesla Model 3

A friend of ours ordered a Tesla Model 3. He paid a $1,000 down payment more than a year ago. When we arranged lunch with our friend, we knew the discussion would be focused on the car, so we pulled up material on special features of the Model 3. When the luncheon took its inevitable turn toward the car, we could tell that our friend was very disappointed that production was behind schedule, and he hadn't heard anything about delivery. When he was at his lowest point, we began feeding him our online discoveries—several features that our friend had never mentioned (for example, the Model 3 automatically syncs with the garage door opener—you do nothing except drive into the garage.). His eyes lit up. He became animated. He even admitted that he had forgotten some of these features or never knew about them. The point of our story? Hidden and add-on value can be quite the energizer. It can lift spirits and embolden buyers.

However, like a missile (or car), it is essential to have a guidance system. That's the second element of Muir's fuel program. Sellers gain best results when guiding the buyer—asking the buyer to "advance" the process in specific ways that point toward a close. In Chapter 2, we refer to these advances as "exit criteria." We can think of sales calls as delivering a sequence of value messages that fuel "advances" and drive the buyer and seller closer to a formalized commitment that addresses the expectations of both parties.[6] The formula is a "give and take." You deliver value messages that energize and motivate a buyer to take "advances" that move the deal forward.

### Commitments: Road Signs for Closing the Deal

In *The Lost Art of Closing*, Anthony Iannarino cites nine commitments that a buyer must make throughout the buying process in order for a seller to close a deal:[7]

1. Serious buyers must be willing to make a commitment of their *time*.
2. Buyers must commit to process to *explore* and discover. What are the roots of the problem?
3. Is the customer willing to commit to *change?* If not, you may be wasting your time.

4.  Buyers must commit to *collaborate*. Without collaboration, it is difficult to agree upon mutually beneficial terms.

5.  A commitment to build or support a process that builds *consensus* is key to a healthy sales process and effective close.

6.  Serious buyers must commit to *invest* financial resources appropriate to the purchase.

7.  *Review* sessions improve transparency.

8.  A commitment to *decide* provides an assurance that the buying process won't die slowly from neglect and lethargy.

9.  Buyers must commit to *execute* or *implement* the product along with the necessary processes that generate benefits for the buying organization.

Think of commitments as "road signs" that alert you to how well the deal progresses and the prospect for closure. The greater the buyer's commitment, the more likely the road will allow you to proceed. Buyer reluctance or indifference for fulfilling a commitment may signal potholes or even mudslides. However, Anthony's book is much more than a list of commitments. He explains that gaining a buyer's commitment means having the right mindset, skill set, and tools to engage and motivate a buyer to make and honor their commitment.[8]

## BARRIERS TO CLOSING THE DEAL

Sometimes a buyer won't make a purchase because they can't. There may be hidden barriers to completing the sale. Perhaps the company is planning to reorganize, and they want the new department head to participate in the decision process. Perhaps the company is understaffed in a couple of key departments. Buyer-centered sellers strive to uncover and understand the decision-making obstacles the buyer faces.

Let's look at four real deal killers and what you can do to address the underlying threat to closing the deal.

Figure 11-2: Four Real Deal Killers

1. **Personal fears can outweigh business outcomes.** Every sales proposal represents change for the buying organization. The larger and more complex the proposal, the greater the change required. Consider a hospital that's mulling a new software suite that embraces patient records, accounts payable and receivable, and performance measures for departments. The ramifications of purchasing a new information system touches a broad spectrum of executives and managers in the healthcare organization.

   Each stakeholder perceives change through a different lens and sees success or failure as it relates to them personally. While your software proposal may provide extraordinary business benefits to the buying organization, it may raise fears and concerns at a personal level among individual stakeholders. "Will the implementation disrupt my vacation plans?" "Will the capital outlay put my pet project on the back burner?" "How will I get up to speed on the new software and its capabilities?"

   **Recommended Action:** Just ask. Before finalizing any negotiation session, probe your customer. "Is there anything that we have discussed or agreed upon that makes you uncomfortable?" "What potential downside concerns you the most?" "Is there any reason you will not recommend our product as the solution of choice?" Probe for anything that might be a hidden personal loss for your customer. Then consider what you (and your proposal) can offer to minimize the threat posed to your customer.

2. **Mistaking agreement for commitment.** Often the sales representative faces a team of stakeholders with input into the negotiation process. If the stakeholders appear to agree on how to resolve points of dispute, and the seller mistakes this consensus for a commitment, the seller can be blindsided. Agreement may not imply commitment.

### Story: Letter of Intent

Several months ago, a close friend shared a story that illustrates the difference between agreement and commitment. His son was a highly recruited football player with multiple offers from Division 1 schools. To sway his son to choose Auburn University (the father's alma mater), our friend shared what he believed to be well-thought-out reasons. For example, Auburn is closer to home and easier for the parents to attend football games.

When the National Letter of Intent Day came, my friend was shocked when his son selected Georgia Tech. "I can't believe it! I thought we were in agreement, and then he selected Tech."

The lesson from this story is that agreement doesn't mean commitment!

The task of the seller isn't just to reach agreement—it's to create a heightened commitment that will support action. When a customer is committed to a provision, he/she is ready and willing to act. The challenge for the negotiator is straightforward: "What do you do if you suspect that one or more parties appear to agree but may be reluctant to act?"

**Recommended Action:** Buyer-focused sellers often conduct focused discussions with stakeholders. They may use a prioritizing exercise to rank order issues or conduct brainstorming sessions to identify options. Focus on the issues of urgency, immediate action, and executive support. The purpose of the discussion is to provide an opportunity for all members to voice reservations and to allow the seller an opportunity to assess their commitment to act. Don't just search for agreement—drive commitment to action.

3. **Any deal is a good deal.** Closing a deal doesn't always mean both sides are winners. Does the seller really understand what the buyer wishes to accomplish in the purchasing process? Are they getting part or all of what they set out to achieve? Is their buying decision defensible to their counterparts and to the executive team? Is the buyer about to make a decision that would expose the buying organization to substantial risk? Often being a good buyer-centered partner means saving the buyer from being blindsided by a decision that could come back to haunt both parties.

   There is an additional implication to the blind spots sellers create with the "any deal is a good deal" mentality. To consummate the deal quickly, sellers may be willing to make concessions and offer discounts. What happens when it's time to extend or renew the contract? The buyer will remember the discounts and concessions and expect the same benefits in future negotiations. A bad deal can ruin the opportunity for future success.

   **Recommended Action:** Consider answering several questions that may help you determine if the deal is a "win-win."
   - Are all "users" (individuals who are likely to be impacted by the buying decision) in agreement with the decision?
   - What might go wrong in the first ninety days that may result in an unanticipated downside risk for the buying organization?
   - Does the "deal" help the buying organization mitigate or eliminate a problem or threat, or does it capitalize on an opportunity?
   - Does the buying organization fully understand the benefits of your solution and when these benefits are likely to accrue?

   Also, is this a good deal for your organization? If you are going to give something, what are you requesting in return? Slow down. Don't turn a good sale into a bad deal by making an unnecessary concession.

4. **Failure to re-qualify the Customer.** Buyer-centered sellers qualify customers at all stages of the buying process. They want good customers, not just good deals. How a customer negotiates the close to a deal is a good indicator of their behavior as a partner. Are they willing to share information? Are they truthful? Do they honor their commitments? Do they make unreasonable or unprincipled demands?

    **Recommended Action:** Many sales teams build a "profile" of the perfect or ideal customer and compare prospects against that profile throughout the sales cycle. Take a close look at your best customers, and reflect on the qualities, attributes, or demographic characteristics that make them good partner material. Qualify your prospects on an ongoing basis—early, late, and often.

## HOW BUYER-CENTERED SELLERS NEGOTIATE A CLOSE

Let's look at the guidelines and best practices that buyer-centered sellers use to close deals. While every close is a process of give-and-take, it can easily turn into "give a little, take a lot." Consider the following guidelines when negotiating elements of the settlement.

1. **"Present your price with confidence."** Body language and tone of voice should exude confidence that your price is fair and equitable. Buyers can become competitive and predatory when they sense flexibility. If they think a seller isn't confident about their price, they will pounce.

2. **"Never give up something unless you ask for something in return."** It's an adage but well used by successful sellers. They avoid setting buyers' expectations that they can get something for nothing. Even if their "ask" is frivolous or without monetary value, ask for something in return.

3. **"Never concede to all buyer demands."** Let's consider a simple close. You are selling a new medical device at full list price. Your buyer

responds by proposing a 5% discount. It's a discount that falls well within your discretion. You feel the adrenalin rush through your body because you know you're going to close the deal quickly. You do your best to mute your temptation to say, "You got it!" Then a little voice says, "Where did that 5% come from?" "Would they accept a 4.5% discount?" "How about 2.5%?" Then your spine stiffens, and you find these words tumbling out of your mouth. "Based on the numbers you have shared with me, your payback with our device is 4 months. After that time, your organization makes a healthy profit for the life of our product. Our price is fair. Sign the deal, and let's get started working together and getting you the financial results outlined in our proposal and agreed upon by you." You're a hero.

4.  **"Never give too much, too quickly, or too often."** Whether it's a giveaway, takeaway, or throwaway, it's important to make your counterpart "work for it." They will appreciate you and purchase more if you make it challenging. You don't want your buyer to think, "That was too easy. I bet I could have gotten a better deal if I had worked it." If you are conceding a provision, test the waters a little. Determine the buyer's flexibility.

5.  **"When confronted with a 'split the difference' recommendation, do the math."** We use a "split the difference" as a tool for resolving personal differences in everyday life. A couple of businesswomen at lunch may "split the difference" rather than calculate an exact bill for each. It's easy, but it may not be fair. Here's why. If we were driving from Phoenix to San Diego, it might be fair to split the driving time: one of us will drive half the way, and the other will drive the remainder. But what if we are 100 miles into the trip and one has driven the whole time? It wouldn't be fair to simply split the remaining driving distance. Many negotiators use "split the difference" after an initial bid has already been offered. If the seller's offer has been very gracious, and the buyer's offer has been miserly, then a split would

benefit the buyer. Do the math. It might sound fair, but it could turn a good deal into bad business.

6. **"Don't be intimidated by extreme anchors."** An "anchor" is the initial price offered by either buyer or seller. Sometimes an extreme anchor is used by one party to force the other to quote a much higher or lower than normal price out of fear of losing the deal. Let's consider this situation. The buyer has done her homework and knows that the list price on the device she wants to buy is $1,000 and that most sell (with a 5% discount) at $950. The buyer has heard stories of people getting it for less but has no way of knowing how much lower the seller is able to go. The buyer says, "I've done my research and don't want to waste time. What if I offer $700 (this is an extreme anchor or 30% discount)? I'm afraid that's the best I can do." The seller says, "I can't even take this offer to my boss. He would laugh me out of the room." "How about $800?" (The seller offers his walk-away price at $800). The seller is beginning to sweat because he's right at his walk-away point with no negotiating room. The buyer says, "I hate to do this, but I'll raise the price to $750, but absolutely no higher." You're dead. You can't go that low; you have no room.

Suppose the buyer says, "Well let's do this: you give me your best final price, and I'll either take it or leave it." The seller says, "The best I can do is $800." The buyer responds, "OK, I'll take it." Do you see what happened? The buyer quoted an extremely low price to create a panic bid from the seller, something lower than he would normally offer. The buyer wanted to test the seller: "Am I getting the lowest offer possible?" The extreme anchor was designed to flush out the seller's walk-away point.

7. **"Respect your walk-away price."** Perhaps the hardest decision a seller can make is saying "no" to a deal. But we've all been faced with deals that are unacceptable and unworkable. Keep close track of where you are in relation to your walk-away price. Tell your counterpart where

you are and why the deal won't work at that price. Be firm, and you may be surprised at how many times you will find that the buyer is just testing your flexibility. Now the pressure is on them to adjust their bid or expect you to walk.

8. **"Keep a record of all concessions, bundles, and trades."** Often buyers and sellers are so caught up in closing the deal, they don't keep accurate records of the transactions. Adrenalin can cause you to overlook things like that. Always control the documentation of your discussions. Include timeframes and any side issues that may have arisen. As you conclude a discussion of any single provision, repeat the written record of your understanding, and gain agreement from your counterpart.

9. **"Be cautious with the future value of money."** It's easy to offer a discount or reduction in future-year pricing when you run out of discount "room" in the current fiscal year. This may sound good to the seller because he/she won't have to deal with the discount this year, but that number may come back to haunt the seller in year 2 or 3 of a deal.

10. **"Is the buyer closing the deal or exploring options?"** Too often buyers give the impression that they are negotiating in good faith when they are exploring the viability of competitive bids. Buyers are asking themselves, "Where can I get the best financial deal?" "How flexible is this seller?" To mitigate this tactic, a seller can offer a discount of "X" for an agreement closed by "Y" date (i.e., today, tomorrow, or this week). The deadline forces the buyer into a decision.

## SELLERS' SECRETS FOR MANAGING A SUCCESSFUL CLOSE

Buyer-centered sellers have a "toolbox" of actions that help them drive the buying process forward. They know when closing a deal is possible or premature. They recognize that closure is a process, not an event. They are patient, probing, and creative. There is no single model for closing a deal...but there are common activities you may deploy to hasten a mutually beneficial deal. Consider the following tactics:

- **Create a problem-solving context.** Closing a deal is about managing change to solve problems. Instead of bargaining, buyer-centered sellers employ a discussion format that promotes an open conversation about interests, concerns, and options. Never close a deal until all obstacles have been addressed.

- **Use questions to identify the buyer's concerns & priorities.** Often sellers make assumptions about a buyer's concerns and interests. Buyer-centered sellers help their buyers list and prioritize their interests. "What are your primary objectives in this deal?" "What are your 'must have' benefits from our partnership?"

- **Test the buyer's flexibility.** Sometimes the most congenial buyer can become stubborn and inflexible over an important concern. Effective sellers understand that the buyer may feel rushed or may feel like they are making themselves vulnerable to unaddressed risks. They use questions, options, and discussion to explore the reasons underlying the buyer's inflexibility.

- **Set and confirm an agenda.** An agenda is a "road map" for discussion. Buyer-centered sellers take responsibility for creating an agenda and checking with their counterpart. "How are we doing?" "Should we move on to the next issue?" "Have we forgotten any concerns?"

- **Explore ways to "expand the pie."** Often a sales opportunity begins with a limited scope of products and services. Top performers look for ways to "expand the pie" and broaden the portfolio of services and products. They take their time and explore the possibility of a bigger deal.

- **Anticipate concerns.** Most concerns that delay or derail a close fall into one of three categories: price, timing, and risk. You should anticipate concerns in each category and prepare a response.

- **Calculate and convey the "cost of inaction."** Many buyers are lulled into inaction by a status quo that hasn't performed to everyone's satisfaction but hasn't failed yet. Be prepared to document the costs of "no change." Discover the internal track record of the status quo.

- **Continue to confirm the "buyer's window."** Sometimes buyers need to be reminded of their internal timelines and due dates. A "buyer's window" is the expected timeframe, from the buyer's perspective, for closing the deal. Buyer-centered sellers continue to confirm the expected timeframe and look for signs that the buyer has lost his/her sense of urgency.

- **Explore multiple offers at the same time.** Top performing sellers recognize the value of multiple offers. Multiple offers provide buyers with choices that prompt discussion. They test a buyer's true priorities. They give the buyer a sense of control.

- **Listen carefully.** Savvy sellers are good listeners. They understand the therapeutic value of engaging buyers in discussion, helping them "talk through" their concerns and prioritize their challenges.

- **Build internal stakeholder consensus.** Work with stakeholders and users to create support. When confronted with complex, high-price purchasing decisions that have widespread ramifications, Executive Buyers are comforted by knowing the decision has strong internal support. Drive consensus.

- **Create a buyer's road map.** The purpose of a buyer's road map is to outline how the product/service/solution will become a part of the buyer's operational system. Specifically, the road map should address:
  - Implementation
  - Ongoing support

- Training
- Timelines
- Benchmarks and measures
- Immediate next steps
- Financial outlay for the buyer

Without some guidance, a buyer (or group of buyers) can drift offline in their planning and implementation.

## Key Points to Remember for Buyer-Centered Sellers

1. Closure is a process of blending the buyer's and seller's expectations into mutually beneficial commitments that are binding.
2. Keep in mind that professional sellers close 50% or less of the opportunities they forecast to win.
3. For more than a decade, the closing rate of professional sellers has been in decline.
4. Typical closing techniques appear to have a relatively low success rate.
5. Deferring the close until the end of the buying process may not be helpful. You risk sticker shock or surprise confrontations that drive the buyer and seller apart.
6. Some traditional closing techniques are "toxic" because they appear manipulative and abrasive to buyers.
7. Deals do not generally close themselves. The buyer-centered seller must guide the process forward.
8. There are five core elements to a close: exchange of expectations, confirmation of timelines, price demands, concession plans, and progress management.
9. Value messages can fuel a buying process.
10. Don't give something unless you are going to get something.
11. Don't concede to all buyer demands; it sets a terrible precedent.
12. When confronted with a "split the difference" recommendation—be very careful, and do the math.

13. Respect your "walk-away price."
14. Keep a written record of all agreements on provisions, terms, and conditions.
15. When contacted to negotiate, is the buyer closing the deal or shopping for a premium price?

## THE SKILL CHALLENGE

In order to become more effective and buyer centered, what skill can you identify from the content in this chapter that requires skill and practice? Please write it here or on a separate sheet of paper.

# ADDENDUM 12: A BUYER-CENTERED SELLER'S CHECKLIST FOR NEGOTIATING A CLOSE

## Understand the Buyer's Expectations
- ☐ Have I uncovered my buyer's expectations?
- ☐ Have I tested the buyer's flexibility on critical issues?
- ☐ Do I understand the buyer's priorities and options?

## Uncover Personal Fears & Concerns
- ☐ Do my buyers harbor fears and concerns about my solution?
- ☐ Are there unaddressed risks that may impact my buyers personally?
- ☐ Have I addressed all issues surrounding implementation and transition?

## Build Commitment
- ☐ Have my buyers been collaborative partners in the buy-sell process?
- ☐ Have my buyers been willing to take actions that move the process toward completion?

## Ensure a Win-Win Outcome
- ☐ Do I fully understand the organizational benefits that are driving the buying efforts?
- ☐ Have I monetized the value of my product or conveyed value in terms the buyer prefers?
- ☐ Does this deal meet the buyers' needs?
- ☐ Is this a good deal for my organization?
- ☐ Is this likely to be a long-term, mutually beneficial partnership?

## Anticipate the Unexpected
- ☐ What internal challenges might arise from purchasing, legal, human resources, materials management, or finance?
- ☐ What steps can I take to initiate contact, provide information, and answer questions?

### Address the Status Quo

- ☐ To what extent is the status quo the buyer's default option?
- ☐ Have I built and communicated a case against "no change?"
- ☐ Have I articulated the hidden costs of the status quo?

### Continue to Qualify

- ☐ What does my customer's behavior during our negotiations tell me about the prospects of a long-term partnership?
- ☐ What obstacles have emerged that may persist throughout the length of our contract?

### Finalize the Deal

- ☐ Define the type of formal agreement
- ☐ Confirm the pathway to the formal commitment

## ADDENDUM 13: THE SIX TYPES OF FORMAL AGREEMENT

Depending upon the industry and the geography the Pathway to the Formal Agreement can require different types of written agreements. Each is described below.

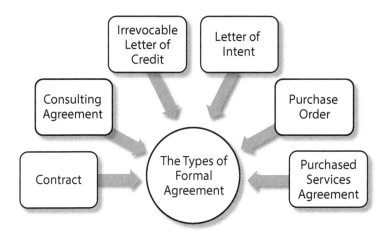

### Contract

A legally binding agreement (written or verbal) between two or more organizations, signed by the appropriate authorized individuals, to undertake or perform a specific task or activity.

Example: The purchase and sale of a home. The buyer and seller each sign a contract.

### Consulting Agreement

A two-sided written contract that outlines the terms and conditions for services to be provided between a Customer and a Consultant. The contract includes general information as well as a confidentiality clause, insurance, non-compete and indemnification agreements.

Example: This type of agreement is often used when organizations hire a consultant to perform research, strategy or human resources work.

### Irrevocable Letter of Credit

A form of credit that is common in international trade that transfers funds from the buyer's bank account to the seller's bank account. It is a firm commitment by the buyer's bank to pay the sellers bank a specified sum in a specified currency provided the conditions included in the document are met within the specified time frame. It cannot be canceled, nor in any way modified, except with the explicit agreement of all parties involved: the buyer, the seller and the issuing bank.

Example: A company that builds small, customized aircraft for private use may require an Irrevocable Letter of Credit before commencing work for a foreign government. Firms use this agreement to facilitate international trade because of the additional risks involved. The irrevocable letter of credit ensures the seller that payment will be made by the buyer's bank if the buyer does not pay the seller.

### Letter of Intent

A letter of intent is often required by a selling organization as assurance that the buying organization is sincere in their intent to award the contract to the seller. In many selling organizations, the legal department requires the Letter of Intent" as evidence that the Executive Buyer has awarded the contract pending proper execution of legal documents.

Example: A software supplier awarded a contract with a "short" delivery timeframe, may expect a Letter of Intent from the buyer to begin creation of the required software package.

### Purchase Order

A type of contract that documents the purchase of goods and/or services. It serves as the legal and binding contract between both parties. Purchase orders are often required by the buyer's organization as part of their internal authorization process. Purchase orders are a verification that funds exist to support purchases.

Example: A purchase order may be required for a department to upgrade and purchase additional printing equipment.

**Purchased Services Agreement**

A service contracted for and performed by a third party rather than an organization's in-house staff. These are very common within healthcare facilities.

Example: This agreement is used when organizations purchase professional services from a company or independent contractor. As an example, a hospital may contract to have anesthesia services provided by an external company.

## ADDENDUM 14: CONFIRM THE PATHWAY TO THE FORMAL COMMITMENT

A close is not complete unless finalized in a manner required by the buying organization. There are three important elements here that the seller must identify.

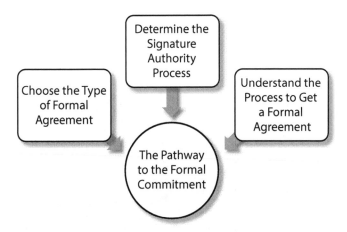

First, which of the six types of formal agreement does the seller desire (See Addendum 13)? Second, what is the signature authority process and who is the final yes? At times, complex selling opportunities need more than one signature for approval before they are submitted to the Executive Buyer for the final yes. This is the individual, or, in some circumstances, a committee, that has the authority to say, "Do the deal." They have the power to release the funds. The third element is for the seller to understand the process to receive the purchase order or execute a contractual agreement. In today's world, most purchase orders are issued electronically. The process includes the order submitted, approval, receiving, tracking, and history. If an organization has a standing order with a supplier, a simple requisition may be all that is required to begin the process.

# Notes and References

## CHAPTER 1: THE FOOTPRINTS OF CHANGE: THE CHALLENGES OF BUYER-CENTERED SELLING

1. Dion Hinchcliffe, "The Rise of the 4th Platform: Pervasive Community, Data, Devices, and Intelligence," *On Digital Strategy* (Blog), 2015. https://dionhinchcliffe.com/2015/05/04/the-rise-of-the-4th-platform-pervasive-community-data-devices-and-intelligence/

2. Nicholas Toman, Brent Adamson, and Christina Gomez, "The New Sales Imperative," *Harvard Business Review.* March-April 2017. https://hbr.org/2017/03/the-new-sales-imperative

3. Toman, Adamson, and Gomez, "The New Sales Imperative."

4. Jordan Bryan, "Make it Easier for Customers to Buy," *Smarter With Gartner* (Blog), 2018. https://www.gartner.com/smarterwithgartner/make-easier-customers-buy/

5. Dion Hinchcliffe, "What is the 4th Platform?" *The Futures Agency* (Blog), 2015. https://thefuturesagency.com/2015/05/11/what-is-the-4th-platform/

6. Various sources have addressed this topic, including The Rain Group, Gartner and Forrester.

7. Eric Almquist, "How Digital Natives Are Changing B2B Purchasing," *Harvard Business Review,* March 2018. https://hbr.org/2018/03/how-digital-natives-are-changing-b2b-purchasing

8. Ago Cluytens, "5 Changes in B2B Buying Behavior You Need to Know About," *Rain Group* (Blog), 2018. https://www.rainsalestraining.com/blog/5-changes-in-b2b-buying-behavior-you-need-to-know-about

9. Brynne Tillman, "The Anatomy of the Modern Buyer and the Modern Seller," *Vengreso,* (Blog), February 16, 2018. https://vengreso.com/blog/anatomy-modern-buyer-modern-seller

10. Brynne Tillman, "The Anatomy."

11. Marissa Grenro, "Winning Over the Modern Buyer," *Marketing* (Blog), June 26, 2018. https://www.highspot.com/blog/winning-over-the-modern-buyer/

12. Toman, Adamson, and Gomez, "The New Sales Imperative."

13. Tim Holdsworth, "Understanding Today's B2B Buyer," Blog, *The Weidert Group Marketing and Sales,* (Blog), 2017. https://www.weidert.com/whole_brain_marketing_blog/understanding-todays-b2b-buyer

14. Tien Tzuo, *Subscribed: Why the Subscription Model Will Be Your Company's Future and What to Do About It,* Portfolio/Penguin, 2018.

15. Frank Cowell, "Do You Understand the Modern Buyer?" *Marketing by the Elevator Agency,* (Blog). https://www.bing.com/search?q=Do+you+understand+the+Modern+buyer+the+elevator+agency&form=APMCS1&PC=APMC

16. Frank Cowell, "Do You Understand the Modern Buyer?"

17. Shawna Sumaoang, "Winning Over the Modern Buyer," *Sales Management Association,* (Blog), 2018. https://salesmanagement.org/blog/winning-over-the-modern-buyer/

18. Shawna Sumaoang, "Winning Over the Modern Buyer."

19. "The B2B Buying Process has Changed…Have You?" *Insite Software,* (Blog), 2018. https://www.insitesoft.com/blog/the-b2b-buying-process-has-changed-have-you/

20. Mark Lindwall, "Why Don't Buyers Want to Meet with Your Salespeople?" *Forrester* (Blog), 2014. https://go.forrester.com/blogs/14-09-29-why_dont_buyers_want_to_meet_with_your_salespeople/

21. Thomas Williams and Thomas Saine, *The Seller's Challenge: How Top Sellers Master 10 B2B Deal Killing Obstacles in B2B Sales,* (Complex Sale Publishing, 2018). 53.

22. Keenan, *Gap Selling. Getting the Customer to Yes: How Problem-Centric Selling Increases Sales by Changing Everything You Know About Relationships, Overcoming Objections, Closing, and Price*, (Sales Guy Publishing, 2018).

23. Toman, Adamson, and Gomez, "The New Sales Imperative."

24. Keenan, *Gap Selling. Getting the Customer to Yes: How Problem-Centric Selling Increases Sales by Changing Everything You Know About Relationships, Overcoming Objections, Closing, and Price*, (Sales Guy Publishing, 2018).

25. Tamara Schenk, "Value Messaging Goes Dynamic and Requires a Dynamic Framework," *Sales Enablement* (Blog), 2015. http://blog.tamaraschenk.com/value-messaging-goes-dynamic-and-requires-a-dynamic-framework

26. Toman, Adamson, and Gomez, "The New Sales Imperative."

## CHAPTER 2: GET CONNECTED: ADAPT TO THE CUSTOMER'S BUYING PROCESS

1. Dave Brock, "Customers Don't Care About Their Buying Journey," *Customer Think,* (Blog), October 21, 2018. http://customerthink.com/customers-dont-care-about-their-buying-journey/

2. Clayton Christensen, *The Innovator's Dilemma: When New Technologies Cause Great Firms to Fail*, (Harvard Business Review Press, 2015).

3. Dave Brock, "Moving Beyond the Chaotic Buying Process," *Customer Think,* October 17, 2018. http://customerthink.com/moving-beyond-the-chaotic-buying-process/

4. Mike Kunkle, "Why Selling Is a Joke," *Richardson* (Blog), January 27, 2014. https://www.richardson.com/blog/selling-joke/

5. Bob Apollo, "The Case for Focusing on Critical Problems," *Inflexion-Point Strategy Partners* March 28, 2017. http://www.inflexion-point.com/blog/the-case-for-focusing-on-critical-problems

6. Bob Apollo, "Complex B2B Sales: Aligning with the Buying Journey," *Customer Think.* August 12, 2016. http://customerthink.com/complex-b2b-sales-aligning-with-the-buying-journey/

7.  Bob Apollo, "The Non-Linear World of B2B Buying," August 28, 2018. https://www.inflexion-point.com/blog/author/bob-apollo

8.  Dave Brock, "Aligning with the Customer Buying Journey." September 21, 2018. *Partners in Excellence* Blog. http://partnersinexcellenceblog.com/aligning-with-the-customer-buying-journey/

9.  Nichols Toman, Brent Adamson, and Cristina Gomez, "The New Sales Imperative: B2B Purchasing Has Become Too Complicated. You Need to Make it Easy for Your Customers to Buy," *Harvard Business Review*, March–April 2017. https://hbr.org/2017/03/the-new-sales-imperative.

10.  Hank Barnes, "Critical Selling Skill-Learning (and Sharing): How Customers Buy," April 17, 2018. https://blogs.gartner.com/hank-barnes/2018/04/17/critical-selling-skill-learning-and-sharing-how-customers-buy/

11.  Mike Kunkle, "Why Selling is a Joke." (Blog).

## CHAPTER 3: THE TORTOISE AND THE HARE: WIN WITH BUYER-CENTERED DISCOVERY

1.  Mike Kunkle, "The Untapped Power of Sales Discovery Skills," *Transforming Sales Results* (Blog), 2015, https://www.mikekunkle.com/2015/04/18/sales-discovery-skills/

2.  Deb Calvert, *DISCOVER Questions Get You Connected*, People First Productivity Solutions, 2013.

3.  Anthony Iannarino, "Your Client is in Discovery Too," *The Sales Blog* (Blog), 1. https://thesalesblog.com/2014/01/08/your-client-is-in-discovery-too/

4.  Kunkle, "The Untapped Power," 4.

5.  Kunkle, "The Untapped Power," 4.

6.  Kunkle, "The Untapped Power," 4.

7.  Kunkle, "The Untapped Power," 4.

## CHAPTER 4: FROM JEKYLL TO HYDE: SELLING TO A BUYER'S BEHAVIORAL STYLE

1.  Jeb Blount, *Sales EQ: How Ultra High Performers Leverage Sales-Specific Emotional Intelligence to Close the Complex Sale,* (Wiley, 2017, 175)

2. Eric Berne, *The Games People Play,* (Dell, 1967).
3. Robert B. Miller and Gary A. Williams, *The 5 Paths to Persuasion: The Art of Selling Your Message.* (Business Plus, 2007).
4. Jim Cathcart and Tony Allessandra, *Nightingale Cassette Series.*
5. William Moultan Marston, *Emotions of Normal People.* (Reprinted by Andesite Press, 2015).

## CHAPTER 5: DIFFERENTIATING WITH VALUE MESSAGES THAT SNAP, CRACKLE AND POP!

1. Corporate Visions, "Create Value," (blog) https://corporatevisions .com/solutions/create-value/
2. CSO Insights, "Sales Management Optimization Study," 2015.
3. CSO Insights, "Sales Management Optimization—Key Trends Analysis," 2016.
4. Robert Kaplan and David Norton, *Strategy Maps: Converting Intangible Assets into Outcomes,* (Harvard Business School Press, 2004).
5. Clayton Christensen, Taddy Hall, Karen Dillon, and David Duncan, "Know Your Customer's Jobs to Be Done," *Harvard Business Review.* 54–62, September 2016. https://hbr.org/2016/09/know-your-customers-jobs-to-be-done
6. Clayton Christensen, "Jobs to Be Done."
7. Neil Rackham and John DeVincentis, *Rethinking the Sales Force,* (McGraw Hill Companies, 2000).
8. Robert Miller, Stephen Heiman, and Tad Tuleja, *The New Conceptual Selling: The Most Effective and Proven Method for Face-to-Face Sales Planning,* (Grand Central Publishing, 2004).

## CHAPTER 6: JEWELS FROM THE JUNKYARD: RESUSCITATING STALLED OPPORTUNITIES

1. CSO Insights World Class Sales Best Practices Report: "Running Up the Down Escalator, 2017," Miller Heiman Group, 2017.

2. Gareth Goh, "Sales Cycle Management: Find Stalled Sales Opportunities Sooner!" Insight Squared (Blog). http://www.insightsquard.com/2013/12/sales-cycle-management-find-stalled-opportunities-sooner/

3. Anthony Iannarino, "Eight Reasons Your Opportunity Stalled," (Blog). https://resources.thesalesbog.com/8-reasons-infographic.

## CHAPTER 7: SCARED STRAIGHT: SELLING TO THE RISK AVERSE BUYER

### Notes and References

1. Demand Gen, "2017 B2B Buyers Survey Report," 2018, Report, p. 2.

2. Demand Gen, p. 2.

3. Demand Gen, p. 2.

4. Gerald Vanderpuye, "Strategies for Introducing New Technologies to Risk-Averse Buyers," *Buyer Deck,* 2017, Blog.

## CHAPTER 8: COLD CASE FILES: ACTIVATING DORMANT LEADS & INACTIVE ACCOUNTS

1. Conversica, "Survey Finds Extremely Poor Sales Lead Follow Up Across Nine Industries," Press Release, *Conversica.* https://www.conversica .com/survey-finds-extremely-poor-sales-lead-follow-up-across-nine-industries/

2. Mike Lieberman, "Why Sales (Not Marketing) is In Charge of Nurturing Dormant Leads," *InBound—The Blog,* 2014. https://www .square2marketing.com/blog/bid/156754/Why-Sales-Not-Marketing-Is-In-Charge-Of-Nurturing-Dormant-Leads

3. John Fakaselis, "Using Campaign Strategy to Revive Dormant Sales Leads," *Access,* (Blog). https://www.business2community .com/sales-management/using-campaign-strategy-revive-dormant-sales-leads-0854961

4. Christopher Lester, "7 Stats That Prove That Email is Here to Stay (and Power Your Business)," *Huffpost,* 2014. https://www.huffingtonpost .com/christopher-lester/7-stats-that-prove-email-_b_5614903.html

## CHAPTER 9: UNLOCKING THE EXECUTIVE MINDSET: SELLING UP

1. Mark Lindwall, "Why Don't Buyers Want to Meet with Your Salespeople?" *Forrester.* Blog. 2014. https://go.forrester.com/blogs/14-09-29-why_dont_buyers_want_to_meet_with_your_salespeople/

2. Ibid.

3. Neil Rackham, *Spin Selling.* McGraw Hill. 1988.

## CHAPTER 10: IS YOUR CROSS-SELLING PROGRAM DRIVING YOU CRAZY?

1. Shopify, "Cross-Selling," *Business Encyclopedia.* https://www.shopify.com/encyclopedia/cross-selling

2. Denish Shaw and V. Kuman, "The Dark Side of Cross-Selling," *Harvard Business Review,* 2012, p. 3. https://hbr.org/2012/12/the-dark-side-of-cross-selling

3. John Senior, Tom Springer, and Lori Sherer, "5 Ways to Increase Your Cross-Selling," *Harvard Business Review,* 2016, p. 3. https://hbr.org/2016/11/5-ways-to-increase-your-cross-selling

## CHAPTER 11: SECRETS TO CLOSING LIKE A PRO

1. James M. Muir, *The Perfect Close: The Secret to Closing Sales,* (Best Practice International, 2015), 1.

2. Muir, *The Perfect Close,* 3–7

3. Muir, *The Perfect Close,* 25–57

4. Robert B. Miller and Stephen Heiman, *The New Conceptual Selling,* (Warner Business Books, 2005), 294–299

5. Muir, *The Perfect Close,* 169–173

6. Muir, *The Perfect Close,* 145–168

7. Anthony Iannarino, *The Lost Art of Closing: Winning the Ten Commitments that Drive Sales,* (Penguin Publishing Group, 2017), 12–14

8. Iannarino, *The Lost Art of Closing,* 204–206.

# Build Your
# Professional Library

## CHAPTER 1: THE FOOTPRINTS OF CHANGE: THE CHALLENGES OF BUYER-CENTERED SELLING

Caponi, Todd. *The Transparency Sale: How Unexpected Honesty and Understanding the Buying Brain Can Transform Your Results.* Ideapress Publishing, 2018.

Dixon, Matthew and Adamson, Brent. *The Challenger Sale.* Penguin Press, 2011.

Franko, Amy. *The Modern Seller: Sell More and Increase Your Impact in the New Sales Economy.* Smart Business Network, 2018.

Keenan. *Gap Selling. Getting the Customer to Yes: How Problem-Centric Selling Increases Sales by Changing Everything You Know About Relationships, Overcoming Objections, Closing, and Price.* Sales Guy Publishing, 2018.

Lindwall, Mark. "Why Don't Buyers Want to Meet With Your Salespeople?" Forrester, September, 2014.

Nick, Michael, J. *The Key to the C-Suite.* AMACOM Press, 2011

Norman, Steven. *Future Proof Sales Strategy: 7 Steps to Rise Above the Chaos, Transform Your Team, and Take Charge of Your Career.* McPhersons Printing. 2018.

Rackham, Neil. *Spin Selling.* McGraw-Hill Education, May, 1988.

Read, Nicholas, A. C. and Bistritz, Stephen J. *Selling to the C-Suite*. McGraw Hill, 2010.

## CHAPTER 2: GET CONNECTED: ADAPT TO THE CUSTOMER'S BUYING PROCESS

Adamson, Brent, Dixon, Matthew, Spenner, Pat, Tornar, Nick. *The Challenger Customer: Sell to the Hidden Influencer Who Can Multiply Your Results*. Portfolio Publisher, 2015.

Caponi, Todd. *The Transparency Sale: How Unexpected Honesty and Understanding the Buying Brain Can Transform Your Results*. Ideapress Publishing, 2018.

Davis, Kevin and Gschwandtner, Gerhardt. *Slow Down, Sell Faster!* 2011.

Franko, Amy. *The Modern Seller: Sell More and Increase Your Impact in the New Sales Economy*. Smart Business Books, 2018.

Johnston, Euen. "5 Steps to Understanding Your Customer's Buying Process." *B2B Marketing,* 2016.

Jones, Shane. "Buying Processes and How to Market Them." *Consumer Marketing,* 2014.

## CHAPTER 3: THE TORTOISE AND THE HARE: WIN WITH BUYER-CENTERED DISCOVERY

Kelly, Mark. "9 Key Insight Categories in the Discovery Process." *Smart Insights (Blog),* 2014. https://www.smartinsights.com/marketplace-analysis/customer-analysis/insight-customer-client-discovery/

Miller, Robert B. and Stephen E. Heiman. *The New Conceptual Selling: The Most Effective and Proven Method for Face-to-Face Sales Planning*. Kagan Page, 2012.

Rackham, Neil. *SPIN Selling*. McGraw-Hill, 1988.

Rackham, Neil. *The Spin Selling Fieldbook: Practical Tools, Methods, Exercises, and Resources*. McGraw-Hill Education, 1996.

## CHAPTER 4: FROM JEKYLL TO HYDE: SELLING TO A BUYER'S BEHAVIORAL STYLE

Asher, John. *Close Deals Faster*. IDEAPRESS Publishing, 2017.

Blount, Jeb. *Sales EQ: How Ultra High Performers Leverage Sales-Specific Emotional Intelligence to Close the Complex Sale*. Wiley, 2017.

Wilson Learning Library. *Versatile Selling: Adapting Your Style So Customers Say Yes*. Nova Vista Publishing, 2003.

## CHAPTER 5: DIFFERENTIATING WITH VALUE MESSAGES THAT SNAP, CRACKLE AND POP!

Konrath, Jill. "Value Propositions Example: Words that get Meetings." *Sales Prospecting* (Blog), 2013. https://www.jillkonrath.com/sales-blog/bid/140981/Value-Proposition-Examples-Words-That-Get-Meetings

Corporate Vision. "Create Value." (Blog) https://win.corporatevisions.com/rs/413-YED-439/images/Solution-Brief-Create-Value-Content.pdf

Hutson, Don. *Selling Value: Key Principles of Value-Based Selling*. Executive Books, 2015.

Osterwalder, Alexander and Pigneur, Yves. *Value Proposition Design: How to Create Products and Services Customers Want*. Wiley, 2015.

Thomas, Julie. *Value Selling: Driving Up Sales One Conversation at a Time*. VVA Publishing, 2006.

## CHAPTER 6: JEWELS FROM THE JUNKYARD: RESUSCITATING STALLED OPPORTUNITIES

Dixon, Matthew and Adamson, Brent. *The Challenger Sale: Taking Control of the Customer Conversation*. Portfolio, 2011.

Kurlan, Dave. "Stalled Sales Opportunities: When Your Prospect is Hiding." (Blog) 2011. http://www.omghub.com/salesdevelopmentblog/tabid/5809/bid/66451/Stalled-Sales-Opportunities-When-Your-Prospect-is-Hiding.aspx

Miller, Robert B. and Stephen E. Heiman. *The New Strategic Selling*. Grand Central Publishing, 2008.

Rackham, Neil. *Spin Selling*. McGraw-Hill, 1988.

## CHAPTER 7: SCARED STRAIGHT: SELLING TO THE RISK AVERSE BUYER

Demand Gen. "2017 B2B Buyers Survey Report." *Demand Gen*, 2018.

Zappulla, Justin. "The Sales Rep's Guide to Dealing with Risk-Averse Clients." *Janek Performance Group*, 2015.

## CHAPTER 8: COLD CASE FILES: ACTIVATING DORMANT LEADS & INACTIVE ACCOUNTS

Blount, Jeb. *Fanatical Prospecting*. Wiley, 2015.

Carroll, Brian J. *Lead Generation for the Complex Sale*. McGraw-Hill, 2006.

Stocker, Mike. "Awaken the Dead! How to Re-Engage Your Audience with Reactivation Campaigns." *Digital Marketing*, 2007.

"To Hell with Cold Calling—3 Steps to Warming Inactive Accounts." *Telesales Master*, 2011.

Ehmann, Lain. "Wake the Sleeping Giant: Reactivating Dormant Accounts." *Selling Power*.

## CHAPTER 9: UNLOCKING THE EXECUTIVE MINDSET: SELLING UP

Nick, Michael, J. *The Key to the C-Suite*. AMACOM Press, 2011

Read, Nicholas, A. C. and Bistritz, Stephen J. *Selling to the C-Suite*. McGraw Hill, 2010.

Parinello, Antonio. *Selling to Vito*. Adams Media Corporation, 1994.

Miller, Robert B. and Heiman Stephen E. *The New Conceptual Selling*. Kagan Page, 2012.

Lindwall, Mark. "Why Don't Buyers Want to Meet with Your Salespeople?" *Forrester*, September, 2014.

## CHAPTER 10: IS YOUR CROSS-SELLING PROGRAM DRIVING YOU CRAZY?

Harding, Ford. *Cross-Selling Success: A Rainmaker's Guide to Professional Account Development.* Adams Media Corp, 2002.

## CHAPTER 11: CLOSE LIKE A PRO

Konrath, Jill. "Help! I Can't Close Sales: 5 Ideas to Increase Your Close Ratio." *Sales Accelerated.* (Blog) https://www.jillkonrath.com/sales-blog/bid/127698/help-i-can-t-close-sales-5-ideas-to-increase-your-close-ratio

Iannarino, Anthony. *The Lost Art of Closing: Winning the Ten Commitments that Drive Sales.* Penguin Publishing Group, 2017.

Muir, James M. *The Perfect Close: The Secret to Closing Sales.* Best Practice International, 2016.

Shonk, Katie. "7 Tips for Closing the Deal in Negotiations." PON, *Harvard Law School,* (Blog) 2017.

Subramanian, Guhan. "Dealmaking: Secrets of Successful Dealmaking in Business Negotiations." PON, *Harvard Law School.*

# Acknowledgments

This book would have never happened without the life and work experiences afforded to both of us. Each job, company, employee, channel member, and customer played a role in our learning, thinking and writing.

We would especially like to thank Nancy Williams and Victoria Hodges for their support and companionship.

We would also like to thank all our reviewers who took the time and energy to provide their feedback and suggestions to improve the quality of our content. Your insight was invaluable, and we can never thank you enough for your tireless work.

A special thank-you to: James Muir, Dave Canham, Joe Galvin, James Welsh, Brenda Irwin, Mickey Neverman, Tamara Schrenk, Mike Kunkle, Scott Marans, Mike Joyce Sr, Dana Palmblad, Bill Golder, Michael Spence, Andrew Lambert, Rick Drake, James Robberstad, Al Kepler, Bob Hatcher, Erin Elsasser, Jerone Jackson, Joe Napolitano, Josh Bennett, Jay Mitchell, Karl Ring, Rich Blakeman, Thomas M. Williams, George Ellis and Heather Williams.

Lastly, we would like to thank you, the reader, for reading our book. We will consider this missive a success if we help you close one more profitable deal, shorten a sales cycle, or increase your win rates.

Good Selling!

# About Us

Tom Williams is the Chairman and Founder of Strategic Dynamics Inc. The firm helps organizations accelerate revenue generation. He is a former Vice President of Worldwide Sales, Marketing & Product Service for an organization that sold high technology medical products and services through a variety of distribution channels. He was also the CEO of two specialty hospitals, the Vice President & General Manager of a medical services division and the President of a medical services company. Tom has a bachelor's degree in biology from the University of Detroit, and Master's degrees in Management (MAM) and Business (MBA) from the Peter F. Drucker and Masatoshi Ito Graduate School of Management at Claremont Graduate University. He is also a registered and certified respiratory therapist. Tom is also a certified facilitator in most of the Miller Heiman Group methodologies, and he sold their services, conducted program facilitation, and provided consulting around their various sales methodologies for over eighteen years. His area of expertise is call planning and execution, opportunity management, negotiation, key account management, funnel management, and sales coaching. Tom is also the co-author of *Selling to Hospitals & Healthcare Organizations: A Glossary of Business Acumen & Personnel* and co-author of *The Seller's Challenge: How Top Sellers Master 10 Deal Killing Obstacles in B2B Sales.*

Tom Saine is a Senior Consultant with Strategic Dynamics Inc. with a Ph.D. in Communication from Northwestern University. He is a former senior executive for ARAMARK Corporation. In his tenure with ARAMARK, Tom served as Associate Vice President for Major Account Sales, Vice President of Client Retention and Vice President of Sales. His background in sales management includes supervising direct sales for the U.S. and Canada, developing the division's strategic plan and creating a master plan for retaining business.

Prior to his years at ARAMARK, Tom was on the faculty of the University of Florida and the University of Denver. Tom has published extensively on group communication, decision-making, negotiation and organizational communication. Tom assists executives in forging strategic sales plans and enhancing the skill sets of their frontline sales team. Tom has extensive sales enablement experience in such areas as key account management and retention, sales strategy, prospecting skills, closing deals and negotiating complex contracts. Tom is co-author of *The Seller's Challenge: How Top Sellers Master 10 Deal Killing Obstales in B2B Sales.*

## Contact Information

Phone: 951-515-8159
Website: StrategicDynamicsFirm.com
E-Mail: TWilliams@StrategicDynamicsFirm.com
E-Mail: TSaine@StrategicDynamicsFirm.com

## Connect with Us!

LinkedIn—Tom Williams: www.linkedin.com/in/thomasjwilliams
LinkedIn—Tom Saine: www.linkedin.com/pub/tom-saine/94/3a/7b6
Twitter: SD_Firm
Blog: http://strategicdynamicsfirm.com/blog/

### Training, Workshops and Speaking Engagements

Strategic Dynamics offers a wide variety of training programs and workshops for sales professionals, leaders, and account executives. Our training media, educational design, and delivery format is engaging and designed to meet multi-generational learning styles and preferences. We blend adult learning principles with interactive facilitation and experiential learning, mini-workshops and role-plays to anchor key concepts and drive comprehension and adoption.

We are available for speaking engagements at local, regional, and national events. To discuss your needs, please reach out to us directly or via info@ StrategicDynamicsFirm.com.

### Free Additional Resources

All the figures, tables, checklists, and other resources shown or listed in the book are available on our website at www.StrategicDynamicsFirm. com. Please feel free to download and use any of the material that you found useful.

We will continue to add additional resources so please check back often to the website.

# Index

# Write a Book Review

Both of us hope that you found the book interesting, informative, and insightful. Our goal was to help you overcome several Buyer's Dilemmas and Seller's Challenges by providing an in-depth perspective to both the problem and the solution based on our years of successful and unsuccessful experiences.

Please share your thoughts on our book with your colleagues by writing a thoughtful review on Amazon. Readers appreciate hearing from their peers if a book is worthwhile to read or not.

As you write your review, please consider the following:

- Was the writing clear, concise, and understandable?
- Was the content presented in an engaging and conversational manner?
- Could you identify with the Buyer's Dilemmas and Seller's Challenges?
- Did the sales stories provide good examples of real-life selling situations?
- Did the Chapter Takeaways provide a good synopsis of the highlights of the chapter?
- Was the content presented in the Addendums helpful?
- What was the one most beneficial takeaway that you had from this book?
- Who could best benefit from reading this book?

- What makes this book different from others in its genre?
- What will you do differently now that you have read this book?

Please consider writing your book review right after reading the book when the information and your feelings are fresh in your mind. Please go to Amazon.com now and write your review! If you enjoyed the book, please spread the word. Tell your friends through social media, in conversations, and via E-Mail.

## ALSO AVAILABLE: OUR FIRST BOOK

If you like what you have read here, please check out our first book.

There is a common question that troubles all sellers at different points in their careers: "So, what do I do now?" It may be uttered out of fear or confusion, but it's that moment of paralysis where they realize they're about to lose an opportunity in which they'd invested so much time to win.

*The Seller's Challenge* identifies 10 of the most frequently cited deal-killing obstacles sellers encounter. The challenge may be selling to change-resistant buyers, deploying a sales plan for a biased and unfair RFP process, selling to committees with numerous stakeholders, competing against an entrenched supplier, or engaging Procurement agents who are obsessed with driving price discounts.

If you look closely, there are caution signs that will guide the seller toward the best course of action. *The Seller's Challenge* is a "tactical field manual" that taps current research, best practices, and real-life examples to help sellers craft action plans that optimize productivity and drive success. It's all about what top-performing sellers do—how they research, plan, and implement activities that maximize their chances of winning.

We will share the harsh realities, myths, data, best practices, game-changing approaches, and guerrilla tactics that will elevate a seller's prospects of winning good business. *The Seller's Challenge* is composed of 10 independent chapters—each devoted to an obstacle that haunts sellers worldwide. The book includes many addendums in the form of checklists and worksheets that simplify the content.

Made in the USA
Columbia, SC
12 September 2019